DEC 2007

MARTHA RILEY COMMUNITY
LIBRARY AT MAHANY PARK
Roseville Public Library
Roseville CA 95678

D1620843

Tea in the City:

London

A tea lover's guide
to sipping and shopping
in the city

Jane Pettigrew
Bruce Richardson

EA ROOMS TEA SHOPS TEA LOUNGES TEA SALONS
HOTEL TEAS CAFE TEAS MUSEUM TEAS

Copyright © 2006 Benjamin Press
All Rights Reserved. No part of this work, in whole or in part, may
be reproduced by any means without prior written permission of the
copyright holder.

BENJAMIN PRESS
PO Box 100
Perryville, Kentucky 40468
800.765.2139
www.benjaminpress.com

ISBN 0-9663478-8-9
Printed in China through
Four Colour Imports

*Cover photo: The multi-striped
Paul Smith porcelain is a feature of tea
at the Berkeley Hotel in Knightsbridge.*

Every effort has been made to guarantee the accuracy
of listings in this guidebook. But in a city that thrives
on renewal, change is constant. Avoid disappointment
by phoning to verify information before setting out on
the tea trail.

Seeing London with Tea on Your Mind

It seems that everyone has a tea story. You know the recollection, 'I had tea at Harrods,' 'I had tea at the Ritz,' or 'We had tea at Fortnum & Mason.'

As the owner of an American tea room for fourteen years, I had countless opportunities to talk with guests about their travels to London. For years, I heard similar stories about the same tea venues repeated again and again. I always suggested to my guests that their London tea experiences might be enhanced by going to places frequented by customers who don't have American passports in their pockets!

Deciding where to take tea in London can be an overwhelming decision for the first-time visitor. The well known tea rooms are still going strong, but the exciting thing about the London tea scene is the new and vibrant look premiering at such venues as Sketch, the Berkeley Hotel, or the Tea Palace. Believe it or not, there are tea rooms that remove the leaves from the pot before bringing it to the table. What a break in tradition that is!

Alas, man does not live by tea alone—even in Britain. Fortunately, there are many attractions to feed the eye and spirit as you walk off those clotted cream calories. From my perspective, it's impossible to spend an evening in London without going to the theatre. I know I can head to the Half Price Ticket Booth in Leicester Square to find great last minute seats at bargain prices.

Trafalgar Square, home of the National Gallery and St. Martin's in the Field, is a short walk south. St. Martin's is the parish church of Queen Elizabeth. There is a free concert every day at noon (and a good chance to rest your weary feet).

A 30-minute tube ride will take you across the Thames to London's spectacular Kew Gardens. I like to spend a quiet morning there strolling the 300 acres that showcase 60,000 species of plants. If all that walking works up an appetite, stop by the Maids of Honour down the street from the Cumberland Gate entrance. It's one of the best informal tea spots in the London area.

London's resplendent churches are always a draw for tourists. These sanctuaries are best experienced by attending one of the scheduled services. There is no better way to end an afternoon than with evensong sung by the men and boys' choir at either St. Paul's Cathedral or Westminster Abbey.

3

No London trip is complete without visiting some portion of Hyde Park. Tour buses often stop only at Speaker's Corner. Try a walk in the park early in the morning when Londoners are jogging and riders are out with their horses. Look for a bronze statue of Peter Pan hidden beside the serpentine lake, or peer into the gardens of Kensington Palace. Top off your morning constitutional with tea and scones at the Orangery beside the palace. It's casual and affordable.

Antique lovers will want to take the tube to Notting Hill Gate on Saturday morning and walk a few blocks north to the market on Portobello Road. Prices are not as good as they once were, but the display of treasures makes for great entertainment. You would be wise to stop by one of London's new tea hot spots, the Tea Palace on Westbourne Grove, which is both a tea room and retail tea shop.

A great hotel afternoon tea is on the itinerary of every London tourist. (Please don't call it "high tea" or the staff will know you are a tourist.) If you're looking for excellence, consider two grand establishments on the southeast corner of Hyde Park. The Promenade at the Dorchester Hotel is one

of the venerable locations for meeting friends for tea. This opulent setting has hosted most of the world's celebrities. A few blocks south, the Lanesborough Hotel looks into the backyard of Buckingham Palace. The Conservatory at the Lanesborough has a high glass roof, graceful chandeliers, and potted palms that make it an oasis in a city that can be overcast and gray. The tea selection is extensive and the pastries almost too beautiful to eat.

Back home, your friends will undoubtedly ask where you had tea in London. You'll want to take delight in reporting your spectacular finds, so put on your walking shoes and grab a tube pass. It's time to travel with Jane Pettigrew and me as we share our favorite London highlights.

The Perfect Time for a Tea Guide

This is the perfect time to offer a tea guide to London, for exciting things are happening here. It is important to direct visitors and, indeed, Londoners to the best of the established and the new tea venues.

Being a capital city, things generally happen first in London. So, any new influences, new movements, and new interests become prominent in our great rambling metropolis before they are noticed elsewhere. For a time, Paris and New York were way ahead of us in the trend towards quality tea rooms and tea retail counters, but it is encouraging to note that London's tea world is beginning to really buzz. The entire world thinks of Britain as a tea-drinking nation and expects to find tea rooms and tea lounges in every village, market town, and major city. But until quite recently, we have struggled to think of suitable venues in London (apart from the top hotels) to recommend to visitors who ask 'Where should I go for a really good cup of tea?'

Working on this guide has given me a chance to tell other people about some of my favorite tea spots and to make sure that they don't miss those hidden treasures that never find their way into the pages of ordinary London guide books. I have been really surprised and pleased on my travels around town to find that some of the hotels which I hadn't visited for perhaps a year or so have made incredible improvements in both the list of teas they now offer and the choice and presentation of all the various tea foods. And, of course, more hotel lounges will gradually realize the interest in tea that is now evident and the opportunities that this offers. They, too, will work to choose a wider range of better quality loose leaf teas for their menus and to devise more exciting ways of brewing and serving tea to their guests.

Some of the places mentioned in this guide do not sell or serve tea but have an important historical link with our past and our traditions, and these links back through time and to other cultures give tea its continuing charm and appeal. Such links are not always easy to find, but I hope that the few listed here will add to your enjoyment of the beverage and its place in our past, our present, and our future.

I wish you fun, joy, and happy times on your tea travels around London.

Tea in the City: London

A tea lover's guide
to sipping and shopping in the city

Steeped in History: The story of tea in London

In the middle of the 17th century, London was England's major port, and it was here that the first shipments of tea arrived, delivered by Dutch and Portuguese merchants. They had set up successful trading agreements with China and regularly sailed the high seas carrying valuable and exotic merchandise.

The first advert for tea appeared in London's weekly paper, *Mercurius Politicus*, in 1658, announcing that the "Excellent, and by all Physitians approved, China Drink, called by the Chineans Tcha," would be offered for sale at the "Sultaness Head, a Cophee-house" not far from London Bridge. But tea was not yet popular. When the directors of the English East India Company required a suitable gift for their king, Charles II, in 1664, they scoured around and made do with a silver casket of oil of cinnamon and some "good thea," which they acquired from officers on Dutch ships.

One city merchant, Thomas Garraway, recognized the opportunities that tea offered and was determined to inform potential customers and persuade them to indulge in this new beverage. His broadsheet, *An Exact Description of the Growth, Quality and Vertues of the Leaf Tea*, was the first detailed document that attempted to encourage new sales. Among its claims: "The drink is declared most wholesome, preserving in perfect health untill extreme old age."

Garraway and his fellow tobacconists, coffee merchants, and general traders purchased their bulk teas in warehouses and sales rooms around the city where goods were auctioned 'by the candle.' By this method, a candle was lit, and when an inch had burned away, the auction hammer was brought down. On March 2, 1774, at the Half-Moon Tavern in Cheapside, the East India Company, which held a monopoly on the importation of tea, put up for sale a total of 2,715 chests of Singlo tea that lay in the company's warehouses near the Thames.

Gradually, tea began to appear in general stores and specialty shops set up by traders such as the Twining family, Mr. Gerry of Eastcheap, Buttons of Covent Garden, Robinson, who traded at the Greyhound & King Arms in Fleet Street, and Mr. Richards, who supplied the Dukes of Bedford at their London residence.

> Bulk teas were auctioned
> 'by the candle.' By this method,
> a candle was lit,
> and when an inch had burned
> away, the auction hammer
> was brought down.

Customers were mostly aristocrats or wealthy civil servants. They or a senior member of their household staff made periodic trips to the chosen store and purchased perhaps a pound of green, Imperial, or Bohea tea. Families who lived outside the capital had to wait until a husband, brother, or butler paid a visit to London and could procure the desired quantity of leaf.

A Love Affair with Tea

Wares

Merchants also stocked porcelain tea bowls, saucers, and pots brought in from China or Japan on the same ships that carried chests of tea. Households equipped themselves with items such as "a box of tin to keep his lordship's tea in coole" or "a red earthen teapot, 6 tea dishes and a sugar box." By 1682, the Dowager Duchess of Dorset owned "two tea pots, twelve blew tee dishes, eighteen white tee dishes, tenn wrought tea dishes, two white tee cupps wrought, one tee table," most likely ordered from London or purchased there.

In those early days, the loose leaf tea was sold direct from the chest into a 'screw' of paper that was often tucked in the top of a box or bag of other goods. Customers could choose from a range that would have included different types and grades - black Bohea (a corruption of Wuyi, the name of the mountains in China where the black tea came from), Bohea Dust, Pekoe, Imperial, Congo, Green Hyson, Green Dust, Bloom Green, and Finest Hyson.

Merchants mixed special blends to suit individual customers, kept note of the recipes, and knew exactly what to mix next time a client called. It was not until 1826 that north London tea

proprietor John Horniman developed the idea of packing a measured quantity of tea into a branded packet. When he decided to use foil-lined paper packets for his Horniman brand, other merchants were reluctant to distribute it, fearing a loss of profits from their own loose leaf blends. Branded packets of tea did not catch on until much later in the 19th century.

Tea consumption grew steadily through the 18th and 19th centuries, with growing imports from new British plantations in Assam, Darjeeling, and Nilgiri, India, and a little later from Ceylon. London steadily grew as the center of international tea trade. Teas arrived from distant ports to be stored, sampled, valued, and auctioned on British soil. It was then sold to British merchants and overseas buyers. Chests of tea were stacked high in warehouses on the north and south banks of the Thames close to Tower Bridge.

Brokering and wholesaling companies operated out of premises at Butlers Wharf beside Tower Bridge (an area now home to smart restaurants, apartments, and shops), Hays Wharf (now Hays Galleria shopping

> By the late 18th century, merchants shelved tea in large tin cannisters to protect it from moisture and vermin. Customers often requested their usual tea by bin number.

mall), Wapping (now very chic dwellings), and wharves along Upper and Lower Thames Street (close to the new Millennium footbridge that links Tate Modern with St. Paul's Cathedral). The auctions were held fortnightly in Mincing Lane, with thirty or more firms selling teas from India and China.

Era of the Clipper Ship

The growth in tea business coincided with the era of the great clipper ships, which could plow their way through the rough seas from China to London faster than any ships before them. In earlier days, East India sailing ships had taken up to fifteen months to make the journey from China to London. The first of the American clippers, launched in 1845, cut the trip to less than eight months.

These beautiful ships were sleek and graceful, stable and capacious, carrying more than one million pounds of tea per voyage. The Chinese stevedores could intricately stack the maximum number of chests into the hold. By one account, they loaded a single ship with 8,000 chests of tea and many bales of silk in less than an hour.

As clipper ships built a reputation for speed, annual clipper races became a popular feature of London life. The tea was loaded in the Chinese port of Fouchow (now Fouzhou) in the middle of June each year and, as soon as the cargo was in place, the anchor was raised and the ship set sail, sometimes leaving port before the necessary paperwork was complete in an effort to beat every rival and become the first ship to reach the London docks. Several clippers would head off on the same tide and then become separated due to hazards encountered on the journey. Crowds in London waited eagerly to see which ship would be the first one home.

News of each ship's progress was sent by telegram – a little like the commentary on a sailing race today but without the advantages of modern technology. As the clippers drew closer to London, sampling clerks from major tea companies often slept in hotels near the docks in order to be able to dash down and collect small quantities from newly-landed chests and reach the tasting rooms by early morning.

The crew of the winning ship was paid five hundred pounds sterling by the owners of the cargo – a princely sum in those days – and the teas fetched a higher price than those arriving on a later tide.

As clipper ships built a reputation for speed, annual clipper races became a popular feature of London life.

By the mid-1800s, tea was being consumed in almost every home in London and indeed in the rest of Britain. Prices were lower than ever before, and most everyone could afford a regular supply. Tea became a symbol of temperance and healthful living among those who were troubled by the widespread con-

sumption of alcohol. Temperance taverns appeared, serving no alcohol, and tea parties became a popular way to raise funds for the Temperance Society.

Charles Dickens described such a meeting in the East End of London in *The Pickwick Papers*: "The monthly meetings of the Brick Lane

MAZAWATTEE TEA. "AND TRUE LOVE-KNOTS LURKED IN THE BOTTOM OF EVERY TEA-CUP." *(From a Picture by G. Sheridan Knowles, R.I.)* MAZAWATTEE TEA.

Branch of the United Grand Junction Ebenezer Temperance Association were held in a large room, pleasantly and airily situated at the top of a safe and commodious ladder. The president was the straight-walking Mr. Anthony Humm, a converted fireman, now a schoolmaster, and occasionally an itinerant preacher; and the secretary was Mr. Jonas Mudge, chandler's shopkeeper, an enthusiastic and disinterested vessel, who sold tea to the members. Previous to the commencement of business, the ladies sat upon forms, and drank tea, till such time as they considered it expedient to leave off; and a large wooden money-box was conspicuously placed upon the green baize cloth of the business-table, behind which the secretary stood, and acknowledged, with a gracious smile, every addition to the rich vein of copper which lay concealed within."

Posters for Tea Festivals appeared on walls and fences around town, attempting to persuade citizens to the temperance view. "Why am I a Teatotaller? First – because it is our Christian duty

to deny ourselves, even of lawful things, to promote the happiness of others. Secondly – because, while no blessing is pronounced upon drinking, God's approval is recorded in favor of abstinence."

The first public tea rooms opened in Scotland in 1875, when Stuart Cranston decided to install a few tables and chairs in his tea retail shop in Glasgow so that customers could be comfortable while trying various leaf teas. His sister Kate went on to open her famous chain of Willow Tea Rooms with the interiors and exteriors designed by Charles Rennie Mackintosh. There are two recreations of Willow Tea Rooms in Glasgow today.

In London, the Aerated Bread Company (the ABC) was the first to recognize the commercial opportunities to be had from serving tea and food to a cross section of the public. Their tea rooms attracted office workers, nannies with the children they

11

looked after, city gentlemen, ladies out shopping, and mothers with babies. A pot of tea was cheap, and all sorts of sweet and savory foods were offered.

As the success of the ABC became evident, other companies selling milk, cakes, tobacco, chocolate, and bread followed suit and opened their own tea rooms. A favorite chain of tea rooms was run by J. Lyons and Co., and an anonymous reporter once wrote: "Lyons introduced to Londoners, and later to the provinces, good cheap food with exceptional smartness and cleanliness; it also gave fresh dignity to the occupation of catering."

Soon there were tea rooms all over London, designed with the comfort of female clients in mind, for this was the first time that women could go out alone or with female friends without having a husband, father, or brother to chaperone them. So, as the suffragette movement was gathering strength and women began to take a more active role in national politics, they could meet to discuss their thoughts and ideas in the tea rooms in a way that would have been impossible in most family homes.

New Mood for a New Century

The turn of the 20th century and the death of Queen Victoria brought a lighter, more frivolous note to British life and a growing passion, especially among the wealthy, for dining out and for traveling. Many of London's five-star hotels were built in the first decade of the century and included a palm court or tea lounge where guests could take tea to the genteel sound of an orchestra or string quartet.

The mood of such rooms was often colonial, with palm trees, exotic plants, and rattan furniture creating a light, elegant ambience. For those with money and leisure time, a day's entertainment was not complete until tea had been taken in the Palm Court at the Waldorf or the Ritz, or in the lounge at the Piccadilly or Claridges.

In 1912, when the tango arrived from Buenos Aires, everyone became intoxicated by the excitement and extreme flirtatiousness of this risqué dance. Ladies suddenly were appearing in public in dance dresses that revealed their ankles, and afternoon tea acquired an eccentrically colorful new element. Tango classes taught the basic steps, and the most confident dancers dressed in their new tango gowns and headed out to take tea at the Savoy or the Waldorf and show what they had learned.

At the Waldorf, tables were arranged around the edge of the white and gold ballroom. Sherry, tea, and dainty tea-time food were served, and the dancers could nibble a sandwich, sip some tea, and then take to the floor. For women who arrived without partners, obliging male dancers dressed as gauchos were glad to swirl them to the moody Argentinian tango.

The joys of tea and thrills of the tango ended with the start of the First World War. Women from all classes went to work driving buses, training as nurses, or doing their bit as members of the armed forces. Tea businesses suffered as many of the young men who had worked in warehouses or offices went off to fight and never returned. Cargoes of tea were lost at sea when British ships were sunk by enemy action, stocks were rationed, and prices rose.

When the Tango arrived from Buenos
Aires, everyone became intoxicated
by the risqué dance. Ladies appeared
in dance dresses that revealed their
ankles, and afternoon tea acquired
a colorful new element.

The National Tea Control was introduced in 1918, and three
grades of tea were sold for a fixed price. But through this war
and the next, it was tea that helped keep spirits up, tea that
comforted and cheered, and tea that was declared by historian
A. A. Thompson to be "England's secret weapon." He said of
tea: "That's what keeps us going and that's what's going to
carry us through – the army, the navy, the Women's Institute
– what keeps 'em together is tea."

By the end of the Second World War, the people of Britain were
poor and food was in short supply. Tea was rationed from 1940
until October 1952, and shoppers went off to the grocer's clutching ration books and coupons to collect their meager supply.
Slowly, the disruptions of war faded, and British tea auctions
resumed in 1952.

Nothing was quite the same, though, as large
areas of London remained devastated by bombing. Even the venerable Waldorf had stopped
using the Palm Court in 1939 when nearby
bombs collapsed the glass roof. Throughout
England, the economy was in a slump, and few
people could afford to visit fancy restaurants or
elegant tea rooms.

Roots of a Tea Revival

In the mid 1950s, new life began to emerge, but it was not derived from British traditions. All things American – dances, music, coffee bars, and juke boxes – grabbed people's imaginations and brought young people out onto the streets. It was a diversion from gray days of the past and a signal that the post-war gloom was ending.

Tea took a back seat, and coffee rose to prominence. Many of the ABC and Lyons tea rooms survived until the mid-1950s, but the onslaught of American influences closed the last remaining

> In the mid 1950s, all things American grabbed people's imaginations and brought young people out onto the streets.

sites. Britons still drank tea at home, and special occasions still were celebrated with tea parties, but for thirty years, London offered no venues to entice families out to tea.

Around 1982, tea began to make a shy and tentative reappearance. In Covent Garden, Christina Smith opened her Tea House, still thriving today. The Ritz and the Waldorf introduced tea dances again, attracting widespread media and public attention. In north London the old dairy at College Farm was refurbished and opened as a delightful tea room (no longer operating), and in Clapham, totally oblivious to all the other small awakenings, a group of friends opened Tea-Time because they thought it would be fun.

Gradually the press heard of all these tea happenings and started writing about the history and ceremony of British Afternoon Tea. People would go out to tea clutching a back copy of a woman's magazine or tourist guide that had written about the tradition in order to see for themselves what all the fuss was about. The Covent Garden Tea House flourished, with crowds pushing their way through the door into the limited space inside to buy loose teas and tea accessories, reservations for tea dances sold like hot cakes, and Tea-Time had long queues every weekend. Britons began rediscovering our heritage and realizing once again what a joy it was to go out to tea.

Interest in tea as a part of British culture has grown steadily. In the 1990s, the Tea Council established the Tea Guild to draw together in one organization all the best tea places in London and around the country. Membership is open to tea rooms and tea lounges judged by tea experts to maintain a high standard of quality in factors including decor and style, food quality and presentation, value for money, and many aspects of tea – range of the tea list, tea quality, brewing standards, presentation, and staff knowledge and attitude.

The Guild offers members assistance with advertising and media contacts, and it generates publicity with annual competitions to find the Top London Tea Place and the Top British Tea Place. The competitions have consistently attracted a lot  of media coverage, prompting many London hotels to devote special attention to their tea offerings. As a result, tea lovers now enjoy a wider range of teas, excellent service, and a host of exciting foods such as sandwiches made with interesting flavored breads, homemade jams and fruit curds, scones flavored with seasonal fruits and nuts, and exquisite pastries that turn afternoon tea into a treat for the eyes as well as the taste buds.

Today, London has several tea venues which are proving that the right product, the right style, and the right approach from staff will attract a loyal clientele. For example, since it first opened with its unusual and eccentric decor, Sketch has attracted top celebrities from the worlds of music, fashion, and theatre.

> Britons began rediscovering our heritage and realizing once again what a joy it was to go out to tea.

At Yauatcha in Soho, booking is absolutely essential if you want to enjoy a pot of their fine Chinese and Taiwanese teas. The Tea Palace in west London hit the news with a bang when the first customers discovered the excellent quality of the teas and the stylish interior. The Moroccan-style Momo is always busy, and the Indian Chai Bazaar attracts its own regular clientele of shoppers from Mayfair and Piccadilly. So many choices!

New life is also being breathed into the tea retail sector. While many supermarkets offer only a short, predictable list of bagged teas, places such as Fortnum & Mason and the food halls at Selfridges, Harvey Nichols, and Harrods offer single-estate teas and unusual blends. Whittard of Chelsea has opened stores in almost every major shopping center, not just in London but all around the country.

The most exciting places to go shopping (not just for tea but for other daily requisites) are the street markets around town. Historic Borough Market at London Bridge, buzzing Camden Lock, eccentric Portobello, and the smaller markets in St. James's churchyard and Piccadilly all have at least one tea retailer amongst the stallholders. Grab your shopping basket, put on some comfortable shoes and head off to seek out these true tea enthusiasts while also soaking up some local color!

London: Orientation 101

Navigating the streets of London can be daunting, even for natives of the city. To help you find that one special tea room - or a cluster of tea shops in a particular district - *Tea in the City* features a pair of maps with color codes for various sections of the city. One map depicts areas in the densely populated heart of London, while the other shows the general location of outlying areas that are home to tea-related venues. The maps are not drawn to scale, and all designated boundaries are approximate. For more specific directions, each tea room entry includes a street address and travel recommendations. At the back of the book, you will find a comprehensive index of tea rooms, shopping venues, and historic sites.

Each listing includes a description of the tea room, hours of operation, street address, transportation tips, and cost rating (£ = inexpensive, ££ = moderate, and £££ = expensive).

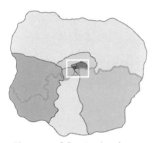

The map of Greater London (above) includes central London and outlying areas of interest.

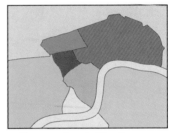

The map of central London (above) shows the general location of city areas cited in this guidebook.

The Royal Boroughs
  Knightsbridge, Kensington, Chelsea

St. James's and Buckingham Palace

Mayfair and Piccadilly

West End and Marylebone

Soho to the City
  Soho, Covent Garden, Bloomsbury, Strand, Holborn, The City

Southbank to Greenwich
  Waterloo, Borough, Greenwich

Western Reaches of the Thames
  Fulham, Putney, Wimbledon, Battersea

Western Hamlets
  Ealing, Chiswick, Kingston, Richmond, Kew

Northern Heaths and Hills
  Camden, Hampstead, Muswell Hill, Harrow-on-the-Hill

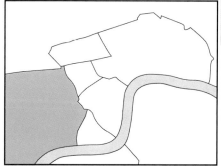

The Royal Boroughs

Knightsbridge, Kensington, Chelsea

These fashionable suburbs once were small villages surrounded by farmland. Today, the area is home to embassies and expensive residences, and elegant squares, parks, and gardens where visitors can stroll. Some of the capital's most sophisticated tea retailers and shops are here.

The Bentley
Neighborhood: Kensington
Harrington Gardens, London, SW7 4JX

The gracious Bentley Hotel is known for its beautiful mosaic floors and extensive use of marble within the building. Adding to the charm, two rooms at this gracious hotel are named after semi-precious stones: the Malachite cocktail bar and the Peridot restaurant where tea is served. As its name suggests, the coloring of the Peridot is green and yellow with pretty touches of gold. The room has the lightness and feminine charm of a French boudoir.

The sumptuous Afternoon Tea offers a welcome change from finger sandwiches, with generous open sandwiches topped with prawns, smoked salmon, and cream cheese and cucumber. Fruit scones are served with organic strawberry jam and clotted cream, and the cake stand is decked with a mouthwatering selection of cakes, pastries, and slices of Victorian sponge.

The Chocolate Tea puts the emphasis on irresistible chocolate goodies, with chocolate chip scones and lots of chocolaty cakes and pastries. A glass of Taittinger champagne turns either meal into a party. You may opt to order à la carte and have just a few biscuits or perhaps toasted crumpets with jam or cheddar cheese and celery. There also are toasted muffins with butter and jam, plus a delicious selection of cakes.

If you're not in the mood for tea-type foods, choose from the list of salads (tomato and feta, Caesar, Nicoise), sandwiches (honey roast ham, prawn cocktail, corn-fed chicken, croque monsieur, roast beef with horseradish and gherkins), and light snacks (omelette or smoked salmon with horseradish and capers). This menu is available every day, 3-10pm.

Loose leaf teas include the Bentley Blend, Darjeeling, Golden Assam, Smoked China, Superior Oolong, Jasmine Pearls, Granny's Garden, Morgentau, Magic Winter, English Breakfast, Earl Grey, Japan Classic, Red Berries, Sports Cup, Lemon Sky, and infusions such as lemongrass, chamomile, and peppermint.

• Afternoon tea served every day in the Peridot, 3-5pm • Nearest tube: South Kensington • Bus: 74 • Tel: 020 7244 5555 • Reservations recommended but not essential • Major credit cards • www.thebentley-hotel.com • Afternoon Tea, Chocolate Afternoon Tea, Champagne Afternoon Tea, tea à la carte • ££

The Jumeirah Carlton Tower
Neighborhood: Knightsbridge
On Cadogan Place, Knightsbridge, London SW1X 9PY

After browsing all the shops of Knightsbridge, wander down Sloane Street to Cadogan Gardens and the Carlton Tower Hotel for a visit to the relaxed and inviting Chinoiserie. The armchairs and sofas are arranged to provide plenty of room between tables, and everyone can have intimate gossipy conversations over their tea without being overheard. Staff members are very good at

Prêt-à-Portea, a fashion themed approach to afternoon tea, is popular at several London tea venues.

"The Paul Smith porcelain that is multi-striped
adds an almost cheeky splash of color
to the expensively stylish room."

The Berkeley Hotel
Neighborhood: Knightsbridge
Wilton Place, London, SW1X 7RL

Step into the foyer of the five-star Berkeley Hotel, and you immediately sense the coming indulgence in style, elegance, beautiful decor, and excellent tea. Prêt-à-Portea is the fashionista's favorite afternoon treat and adds a twist to British tradition. Instead of sandwiches, whet your appetite with miniature crostinis and tiny savory skewers. Then enjoy the smile-provoking selection of cakes and pastries inspired by the fashion collections of top world designers. Nibble your way through an Alberta Ferretti chocolate glitter bow dress or a Dolce & Gabbana white feather coconut cream. There's a John Galliano lace mint cake, a pink-bow vanilla Yves Saint Laurent handbag, and a Dior monochrome chocolate panna cotta.

The sweets threaten to steal the spotlight, but you're bound to admire the Paul Smith porcelain that is multi-striped and touched with gold (featured in this guidebook's cover photo). It adds an almost cheeky splash of color to the expensively stylish room with its muted mahogany tones and earthy soft browns and beiges.

The tea selection includes English Breakfast, Jasmine, Earl Grey Blue Flower, Chai Spice, Organic Assam, Ceylon, Lapsang Souchong, and more.

An à la carte version of Prêt-à-Portea is available, but you must order this when you book with the Caramel Room. You can order up to nine savories or nine fancy cakes with a pot of tea.

• Afternoon Tea and Prêt-à-Portea served every day 2-6pm (see details above about ordering in advance) • Nearest tubes: Knightsbridge, Hyde Park Corner • Buses: 38, 52, 73, 436 • Tel: 020 7235 6000 • Reservations recommended • Major credit cards • www.the-berkeley.co.uk • £££

21

looking after their guests, and the resident harpist adds a soothing touch.

The lounge area is open all day for breakfast buffet, light lunchtime snacks, afternoon tea, and evening drinks. Teas include English Breakfast, Earl Grey, Assam, Jasmine, Ceylon, Lapsang Souchong, China Oolong, Darjeeling, Gunpowder, Peach, Four Red Fruits, Strawberry, lemon-flavored green, and various fruit and herbal infusions. The Knightsbridge Afternoon Tea consists of finger sandwiches, raisin and plain scones with Devonshire clotted cream and strawberry and apricot jam, French pastries, and fruit cake. The Carlton Tower Afternoon Tea adds the tempting sparkle of pink champagne.

• Afternoon tea served in the Chinoiserie every day, 3-6pm • Nearest tubes: Knightsbridge, Sloane Square • Buses: 19, 22, 137, C1 • Tel: 020 7235 1234 • Reservations recommended • www.jumeirahcarltontower.com • Major credit cards • Knightsbridge Afternoon Tea, Carlton Tower Afternoon Tea, Afternoon Tea à la carte, tea by the pot • £££

Harrods Georgian Restaurant
(in Harrods Department Store)
Neighborhood: Knightsbridge
87-135 Brompton Road, Knightsbridge, London, SW1X 7XL

To reach this popular tea lounge, take the escalator inside Harrods to the fourth floor and follow signs to the restaurant. After a short flight of steps, you will find yourself surveying a vast art nouveau room with a glass ceiling and contented

Charles Henry Harrod rented a small shop in Knightsbridge in 1834 and turned it into a thriving business. Today, Harrods is one of the world's most famous department stores.

tables of tea drinkers enjoying the buzz of a sociable afternoon tea. A pianist plays lilting melodies in the background while smart waiters in black and gold striped waistcoats deliver countless pots of tea and silver cake stands to the tables.

The Traditional Tea offers the usual sandwiches, raisin scones, and Harrods famous pastries, along with a selection of top quality teas from China, India, and Sri Lanka. If you choose the Georgian Tea, the food is the same, but you will be brought three very fine teas to enjoy with your meal. Darjeeling Okayti Treasure Tea is the best from that estate, the organic white tea from Ambootia is delicate and 'reminiscent of a spring breeze,' and the Assam Jamguri Golden Blossom is made from the buds and leaves of hundred-year-old bushes. On celebratory occasions, add a glass of Harrods champagne to either of the set teas.

Don't miss **Harrods food hall** on the ground floor of the department store. This sumptuous hall offers every kind of consumable treat, and the selection of teas offered in the left hand section of the Chocolate Room must be the widest ranging in Britain. The large red and green caddies behind the counter hold supplies of loose teas from China, Japan, Taiwan, from all the top plantations in Darjeeling, Assam, Nilgiri, and Sri Lanka, green teas, oolong teas, white teas, blended teas, organic teas, and flavored teas. Shelves all around hold an excellent choice of other branded teas, gift boxes, wooden caddies from Sri Lanka, teabags, fruit and herbal infusions, and decorative sugar cubes with sugar flowers on top.

• Afternoon tea served in the Georgian Restaurant every day, 3:15-5:30pm (last orders) • Nearest tube: Knightsbridge (Harrods exit) • Buses: 9, 10, 19, 52, 74, 414 • Tel: 020 7730 1234 • Reservations recommended • Major credit cards • www.harrods. com • Afternoon Tea, Georgian Afternoon Tea, Champagne Afternoon Tea • ££

Harvey Nichols Fifth Floor Restaurant

Neighborhood: Knightsbridge
109-125 Knightsbridge, London
SW1X 7RJ

To find the airy, light room that is the Harvey Nichols restaurant, enter the store by the main door on Sloane Street, turn right, and take the lift to the fifth floor. Follow signs to the restaurant and wait to be seated. The modern decor here is simple but stylish, creating a chic setting for a very welcome pot of tea when your legs decide that you've been shopping too long. For a very reasonable price, be tempted by the Afternoon Tea with its sandwiches, scones, straw-

berry tart, pecan chocolate slice, and Florentine with a pot of tea, or choose from the à la carte menu of sandwiches filled with smoked salmon, cucumber or egg mayonnaise and cress, or from the selection of tarts, pies, and cakes. A slice of Belgian chocolate tart or a wedge of carrot cake with a pot of Darjeeling, Jasmine, or Assam will quickly restore flagging energy, setting you up for another hour or so of covetous browsing.

The classy **Harvey Nichols food hall** is adjacent to the restaurant, so after tea you can purchase tins or packets of loose tea or teabags, plus all the ingredients you need for supper. The open metal stacks of shelves hold a good selection of Harvey Nichols' own label black, green, and flavored teas, plus teas by other names such as Taylors of Harrogate, Williamson & Magor, and SIP organics.

• Afternoon tea served in the restaurant every day, 3:30-6pm • Nearest tube: Knightsbridge (Sloane Street exit) • Buses: 9, 10, 19, 52, 74, 137 • Tel: 020 7823 1839 • Reservations possible but not essential • www.harveynichols.com • Major credit cards • Afternoon Tea, tea by the pot • £

Kensington Palace
Neighborhood: Kensington
Kensington Palace, Kensington Gardens,
London W8 4PX

Through the centuries, Kensington Palace has been the home of several British kings and queens. Originally a private country house, it was converted into a royal palace by Christopher Wren for King William III and his wife Mary. The house was the birthplace and childhood home of Princess Victoria until she became Queen in 1837. Victorian writer Leigh Hunt observed that this palace was a perfect place for tea because "the reigns that flourished here were all tea-drinking reigns ... and if the present queen does not reign there, she was

born and bred there." The most famous of recent royal residents was Princess Diana, who lived at Kensington 1981-97.

The Orangery, set to the left of the main entrance to the Palace, is long and strikingly palatial with a white interior. There are south facing windows along one wall, allowing a flood of daylight. In keeping with the conservatory feel of the room, the chairs and tables are black open metalwork. A certain elegance is brought to the dining experience by the crisp white linen tablecloths and delicate fresh flowers that decorate each table.

As you go in, you will be tempted by the mountain of scones and the spread of yummy looking cakes on the serving counter. Once seated, you may order pots of tea, cakes and scones à la carte, or choose the English Tea (cucumber sandwiches, carrot cake, and tea), the Orangery Tea (cucumber sandwiches, a scone with cream and jam, a slice of Orangery sponge cake, and tea), or the posh Champagne Tea (a glass of champagne, smoked salmon sandwiches, a scone with cream and jam, a slice of rich Belgian chocolate cake, and tea).

The tea list is limited. Earl Grey, English Breakfast, and a few infusions are available in bags. Lapsang Souchong, Orange Blossom, Assam, and Darjeeling are brewed loose leaf in white pots.

Upon entering the Orangery at Kensington Palace, you will be tempted by the mountain of scones and the spread of yummy looking cakes on the serving counter.

• Afternoon tea served in the Orangery every day. Hours are 10am-6pm from March 1-Oct. 31. Hours are 10am-5pm from Nov.1-Feb.28. • Nearest tubes: Kensington High Street, Notting Hill Gate • Buses: 70, 94, 148, 390 to Bayswater Road or 9, 10, 49, 52, 70 to Kensington High Street • Tel: 020 7938 1406 • www.hrp.org.uk • Major credit cards • English Tea, Orangery Tea, Champagne Tea, tea by the pot • ££

Milestone Hotel
Neighborhood: Kensington
1 Kensington Court, London, W8 5DL

The Milestone Hotel takes its name from an old cast iron milestone that stands in its original position within the hotel's boundary. The original dwelling on this site, Kensington House, was built around 1689, and residents have included a man who claimed to be Shakespeare's grandson, a mistress of King James II, and a governess to the daughters of King George II. The original house served variously as an academy for young gentlemen, a Jesuit school, and a private lunatic asylum, but

(continued on page 28)

"With such a long and colorful history, it is little wonder that the Lanesborough has the ambience of a grand house where everyone is comfortable and well looked after."

The Lanesborough Hotel

Neighborhood: Knightsbridge
Hyde Park Corner, London SW1X 7TA

The Lanesborough Hotel, just across the road from Hyde Park, was once the country retreat of the second Viscount Lanesborough. His home became St. George's Hospital in 1733, but it was demolished and rebuilt around 1828. In subsequent years, the building stood empty before finding new life as a fashionable hotel. With such a long and colorful history, it is little wonder that the Lanesborough now has the quietly efficient ambience of a grand house where everyone is comfortable and well looked after.

Tea is served in the Conservatory with its domed glass roof that filters in generous amounts of soft light. Gothic arches to the side are hung with Tiffany-style lamps and lanterns. Despite the very English setting, the overall theme is Chinese. You'll see tall Chinese containers and large silver samovars that were once used to brew tea. Around the room, vast planters overflow with exotic palms, ferns, and orchids that give a sense of intense luxury and indulgence. Little wonder that this room has become a favorite place for fashion designers to show their collections.

Afternoon tea offers a list of teas specially chosen for the hotel by Malcolm Ferris Lay, whose family has been connected with the tea trade since 1842. The menu includes Lanesborough Afternoon Blend (a mixture of Darjeeling, Assam and just a hint of Rose Congou), Lapsang Souchong, Earl Grey Blue Flower, Rose Petal, Darjeeling, Lychee, Ceylon Orange Pekoe, strawberry flavored tea, and a few fruit infusions. The Lanesborough Tea is a selection of finger sandwiches, tea cakes, scones with jam and clotted cream, English tea breads, and pastries. The Belgravia Tea adds strawberries and cream, plus a glass of Taittinger or other superior champagne.

• Afternoon tea served every day • Nearest tube: Hyde Park Corner • Buses: 9, 14, 19, 22, 36, 38, 436 • Tel: 020 7259 5599 • Five-star hotel serving Afternoon Tea in the Conservatory • www.starwoodhotels.com/stregis • Reservations recommended • Major credit cards • Afternoon Tea, Lanesborough Tea, Belgraveia Tea, tea by the pot • £££

don't worry about any distressed spirits that may still roam within the walls; the first house and a second one were demolished to make way for a hotel in 1922.

The Park Lounge has clear, uninterrupted views of Kensington Gardens and provides an elegant and restful setting for tea. You can choose the traditional Afternoon Tea that offers sandwiches, freshly baked scones with Devon clotted cream and preserves, and French pastries. The Milestone Champagne Tea adds a glass of bubbly. Afternoon Seduction turns the traditional tea into a feast by adding fruit cake, strawberries and cream, and, not just a glass, but a half bottle of champagne. The Little Prince and Princess Tea is designed for small visitors who may not like tea but will love tea treats with extra chocolate truffles and hot chocolate.

For tea lovers, there is English Breakfast, Darjeeling, Assam, Lapsang Souchong, Earl Grey, green tea, lemon tea with peel, spice flavored tea, black caramel and chocolate flavored tea with little white chocolate hearts, decaffeinated tea, and various herbals.

• Afternoon tea served every day, 3-6pm, in the Park Lounge and the Conservatory or privately in the Windsor Suite for parties of 15 or more • Nearest tube: Kensington High Street • Buses: 9, 10, 52 • Tel: 020 7917 1000 • Major credit cards • www.milestonehotel.com • Afternoon Tea, Champagne Afternoon Tea, Afternoon Seduction, Little Prince and Princess Tea, Cream Tea, tea by the pot • ££

The teapoy became popular around 1800 as a table holding receptacles for tea.

The Tea and Coffee Plant
Neighborhood: Notting Hill
180 Portobello Road, London, W11 2EB

This funky, lively coffee bar is right in the heart of Portobello market and attracts a mixed clientele who like their tea and coffee organic and fairly traded. On a Saturday, it is packed throughout the day, sometimes making it difficult to get to the tea shelves. But push your way through, and on your right you will find a whole selection of bagged and loose organic teas and herbals that include Ceylon, Assam, Fukujyu Sencha, Formosa Gunpowder, English Breakfast, Earl Grey, Green Earl Grey, Darjeeling, Jasmine, Lapsang Souchong, decaffeinated tea, rooibos, maté, various flavored green teas, and lots of herbals – lemon verbena, St. John's Wort, peppermint, ginseng, chamomile, and a detox mixture. The store also stocks organic chocolate, flavored syrups, and coffees.

• Mon.-Sat. 8am-6:30pm, Sun. 10am-5pm • Nearest tubes: Notting Hill, Ladbroke Grove • Buses: 23, 52 • Tel: 020 7221 8137 • Organic coffee bar selling retail packs of organic and Fair Trade tea • Major credit cards • www.coffee.uk.com • £

Victoria and Albert Museum

Neighborhood: Kensington
Cromwell Road, South Kensington, London,
SW7 2RL

This marvelous museum (a personal favorite) can fill a pleasant day with learning, looking, shopping, eating, and drinking. It includes quite a few tea-related galleries. On the ground floor, the China room has a small display of porcelain, enamelled, and Yixing earthenware teapots, bowls, tea bowl stands, and tea jars. The Japan room next door has wares for the preparation of Sencha, Usucha (thin tea), Koicha (thick tea), and Trekaiseki (the meal that accompanies tea). Water vessels, lacquer tea jars, and boxes are on display, along with caddies, bowls and dishes, tea bowl stands, and food boxes. On Level 3, you will find Whiteley's Silver Gallery with displays of teapots, kettles, caddies, cutlery, and strainers. In the British galleries (just up the stairs to your left inside the main entrance on Cromwell Road), you will find various tea-related objects and brewing equipment. One small room (52B) has a tea-drinking tableau arranged behind glass. Admission to the museum is free.

When the time comes for rest and refreshment, you can get a pot of tea and something to eat in the cafeteria, located in the basement of the Henry Cole wing at the back of the museum. The loose leaf teas are brewed in chummy white pots with infusers so you can control your brewing time. Take an extra saucer to hold the infuser when your tea is ready. The tea list includes English Breakfast, Earl Grey, Jasmine, Rose of the Orient, the Warner Blend (Lapsang and Ceylon), Afternoon Blend, and lemon flavored green. Food choices include hot meals, salads, sandwiches, cakes, scones, pastries, and bars of Valrhona chocolate. The tea is excellent, the room (broken up into intimate spaces by huge pillars) is vast enough to always have empty places for newcomers, and it provides the ideal place to chat, read, or rest.

• Museum and cafeteria open every day 10am-5:45pm. Additional hours until 10 pm every Wed. and the last Friday of each month • Nearest tube: South Kensington • Buses: 14, 74, 414 • Tel: 020 7942 2000 • www.vam.ac.uk • £

The Victoria and Albert Museum (known as The V&A) was founded in 1852 as the South Kensington Museum and renamed in 1899 in honor of Queen Victoria and her late consort Albert. Queen Victoria reigned for more than 63 years (1837-1901), longer than any other British monarch.

> "A fusion of Asian and modern European style creates a calm, restful room, and the panoramic view of Hyde Park completes the setting."

Mandarin Oriental Hyde Park

Neighborhood: Knightsbridge
66 Knightsbridge, London, SW1X 7LA

The opulence of the Mandarin Oriental Hotel is evident in the marble that lines the entrance foyer. Enjoy it as you head for the Park, a combination of tea lounge and restaurant where a fusion of Asian and modern European style creates a calm, restful room full of neutral and earthy colors. A panoramic view of Hyde Park completes the setting.

Traditional tea is served on an elegant silver cake stand, and places are set with pure white china plates that are decorated with a delicate blue leaf motif. The feast of sandwiches is supplemented by scones with rose petal jelly or strawberry jam, and pastries. Turn your tea into a celebration with a glass of Pommery Brut Rosé or Dom Perignon champagne. The tea list includes Darjeeling, oolong, Georgian, China tea from Anhui province, Pelham Mixture of China black and Jasmine, Assam, Earl Grey, Lapsang Souchong, Lotus Flower, Mango India, Spiced Ceylon, and vanilla black.

• Afternoon tea served in the Park lounge every day, 3-6pm • Nearest tube: Knightsbridge (Knightsbridge/Sloane Street exit) • Buses: 9, 10, 52, 74, 137, 414 • Tel: 020 7235 2000 • Reservations recommended • Major credit cards • www.mandarinoriental.com • Afternoon Tea, tea by the pot • £££

Queen Mary was betrothed to her Dutch cousin, William, as a matter of foreign policy. This statue of King William III of Orange stands at the gate of Kensington Palace, where he resided until 1702. The Dutch Royal House of Orange received the first Chinese pekoe tea brought by the East Indies Company to Holland, later promoted as Orange Pekoe. Thus, the world's best known grade of tea was born.

Shopping Sites for Tea Lovers

Whittard of Chelsea, Kings Road
Neighborhood: Chelsea, South West London
184 Kings Road, Chelsea, London, SW3 5XP

Here at the heart of London's fashion street, Whittard concentrates more on quality chocolates and gift items than on their everyday tea and coffee. Children hover goggle-eyed over the display of novelty chocolates. As one ten-year-old described the experience: "Now, I'm in heaven." The shop is long and narrow, like an Aladdin's cave full of tempting treats.

• Mon.-Sat. 9am-6pm, Sun. 11am-6pm • Nearest tube: Sloane Square • Buses: 11, 22, 211, 319 • Tel: 020 7376 4986

Whittard of Chelsea, Bayswater
Neighborhood: Bayswater, S W London
33 Whiteleys, Queensway, Bayswater, London, W2 4YQ

• Mon.-Sat. 9am-9pm, Sun. 11am-6pm • Nearest tube: Queensway • Buses: 7, 23, 70 • Tel: 020 7243 6089

Whittard of Chelsea, Kensington High Street
Neighborhood: Kensington, South West London
209 High Street, Kensington, London, W8 6DB

• Mon.-Sat. 10am-7pm, Sun. 11am-6pm • Nearest tube: High Street Kensington • Buses: 9, 10, 27, 49, 328 • Tel: 020 7937 5569

Whittard of Chelsea, Knightsbridge
Neighborhood: Knightsbridge, S W London
203/205 Brompton Road, Knightsbridge, London, DSW3 1LA

• Mon.-Sat. 10am-7:30pm, Sun. 10am-7pm • Nearest tube: Knightsbridge • Buses: 14, 74, 414 • Tel: 020 7581 4767

The southwest corner of Hyde Park at Kensington Palace is a welcoming place to stroll in the morning or afternoon, filled with flower gardens, statuary, and views of the London skyline.

Yumchaa, Portobello Road Market
Neighborhood: Kensington
Portobello Road (Ladbroke Grove End), London, W10

Yumchaa is a dynamic young tea venture run by high-energy partners, Trinh Hoang, and her friend, Sean. In their shop and market stalls they display teas so that customers can see, smell, and assess the leaf and other ingredients. The Yumchaa teas are unusual flavored blends of black, green, rooibos, and white teas, each with a clever name: Sweet Secret, Notting Hill, Chelsea Chai, Mango Sunrise, Adventure, Ooh-la-la, Caramel Sweetheart, Enchanted Forest, Ginseng Guardian, and many more.

• Sat. 9am-6pm • Nearest tubes: Ladbroke Grove, Notting Hill Gate • Bus: 52 • Market stall selling loose leaf teas and infusions • Cash • www.yumchaa.co.uk

A Cup of Royal History

Cups and saucers of the Victorian age tended to be larger than those we see today. Often, the hot tea was poured from the cup into the deep saucer, allowing the heat to dissipate. When the tea reached the desired temperature, it was quite acceptable to drink from the saucer.

One of the earliest cities to make English porcelain was Worcester, located at the western edge of the Cotswolds. By 1789 the quality of the work at the Worcester Porcelain Manufactory was held in such high esteem that King George III granted the company a prestigious Royal Warrant as manufacturers to their majesties. Thus the word Royal was added to the name. While its rivals of the period gradually disappeared, Royal Worcester Porcelain became world famous. The company is now one of the largest manufacturers of bone china and porcelain in England.

This elegant 19th century Royal Worcester cup has a fanciful hand-painted handle in the form of a colorful butterfly.

"This classy and chic tea room is attracting groups of young people, dressed in their best, who come to enjoy the civility and charm of tea time."

Tea Palace

Neighborhood: Notting Hill
175 Westbourne Grove, London, W11 2SB

Tara Calcroft devoted a great deal of time to planning and research before she opened the Tea Palace in 2005. Her attention to detail shows in the very high standard she has achieved. The tea room and shop are quite beautiful with their regal purple and white theme, specially designed carpet with the company's crown motif, wallpaper with a subtle white doiley print, and elegant white porcelain. This is as classy and chic a tea room as you could hope to find, and it is interesting that it immediately started attracting groups of young people, dressed in their best, who come to enjoy the civility and charm of tea time.

The list of teas served in the tea room and for sale at the retail counter totals more than 100 and includes many single estate teas. There are outstanding selections from China, (Yunnan Imperial, Black Pearls, Golden Needles), India (Assam Mangalam, Darjeeling Autumnal, Darjeeling Second Flush Castleton), and Sri Lanka (organic Ceylon Koslanda, Ceylon Silver Tip). You'll also find Japanese greens, China whites, greens, pouchongs and oolongs (Gu Zhang Mao Jian, White Peony with Pink Rosebuds, Organic Super Dao Ren, Organic Gunpowder), and various decaffeinated blacks and greens. Try one of the unusual blends (Builder's Brew, Russian Taiga, Organic Lavender Grey) or some flavored blacks (Mistral, Winter Whispers, Paradise Found), flavored greens (Lemon Shimmer, Royal Star, Blue Sky), or various jasmines.

When any of these teas is ordered in the tea room, the leaves are carefully brewed in the kitchen using infusers and timers. The pot of perfect liquor is then delivered to the table. Because Tara believes in helping people understand more about tea, a tiny white porcelain dish is also delivered to the table with just a pinch of the dry leaf of the particular tea that has been chosen.

Afternoon Tea is brought to the table on a silver cake stand. It features sandwiches, excellent scones with preserves and clotted cream, and a selection of pastries. The entire service is thoughtfully and graciously performed, and it is not surprising that Tara and her shop are attracting a good deal of attention from the media, from visiting tea lovers, and from regular local customers who are lucky to have this on their doorsteps.

• Afternoon tea served Mon.-Sun. 3-7pm; lunch Mon.-Fri. noon-3pm; brunch Sat.-Sun. 10am-3pm, and dinner Wed.-Sat. 7:30pm • Nearest tubes: Notting Hill Gate, Queensway • Buses: 7, 23, 70 • Tel: 020 7727 2600 • Tea retail area open Mon.-Sun. 10am-6:30pm • Reservations for tea not possible. Call or e-mail (info@teapalace.co.uk) for party and group bookings • Major credit cards • www.teapalace.co.uk • Afternoon Tea, tea à la carte, tea by the pot • ££

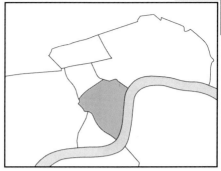

St. James's and Buckingham Palace

A wander through this aristocratic part of town takes visitors past Buckingham Palace and St. James's Palace, through the green slopes of St. James's Park and up into some of central London's narrowest shopping streets in St. James's itself. Nearby are several quality hotels where traditional afternoon tea is served and where guests can catch their breath, ready for more exploring.

The Goring Hotel
Neighborhood: Victoria
Beeston Place, Grosvenor Gardens, London,
SW1W 0JW

Although the Goring Hotel is set just around the corner from Victoria Station, one of London's busiest connection points for trains and coaches, it is rather like a country house hotel where there is a calm, focused attitude from the staff and a very courteous, helpful approach. Those standards were set as long ago as 1910 when O. R. Goring, grandfather of the current owner, opened the hotel.

If you visit for tea today, you will notice a collection of small woolly sheep beside the fireplace in the drawing room. Why are they there? Well, they are George Goring's slightly eccentric way

of helping his visitors (who travel a lot and stay in a lot of different hotels) know exactly where they are. When they see the sheep, guests know that they are in the comforting and comfortable care of the Goring.

Afternoon tea is served in the drawing room or the Terrace, and you can have a full traditional set tea or order tea and food à la carte. The set tea consists of triangular sandwiches on white and brown bread filled with smoked salmon, beef and tomato, egg mayonnaise and cress, and herbed cream cheese and cucumber. You'll also get plain and fruited scones with Devonshire clotted cream and preserves, plus a plateful of small pastries and generous slices of fruit cake and sacher torte with chantilly cream. The tea list includes Goring Special Blend, Assam, Darjeeling, Lapsang Souchong, Earl Grey, English Breakfast, Keemun, Jasmine, and a few infusions.

• Afternoon tea served in the lounge and the Terrace every day, 3:30-5pm • Nearest tube: Victoria • Buses: 2, 36, 185, 436 • Tel: 020 7396 9000 • Reservations recommended • Major credit cards • www.goringhotel.co.uk • Afternoon Tea, tea by the pot • ££

Cream Tea usually consists of a couple of scones with clotted cream and jam, accompanied by a pot of tea, an affordable break that can be enjoyed anytime of the day.

Rubens at the Palace
Neighborhood: Victoria
39 Buckingham Palace Road, London, SW1W 0PS

Located opposite Buckingham Palace a short stroll from St. James's Park, the Mall, and Green Park, the Rubens is a very traditional hotel and serves a traditional Afternoon Tea. The Original Crumpet Tea adds toasted crumpets to the sandwiches and cakes instead of scones (great in winter or when you've overdosed on scones). While you tuck into your sandwiches, you can enjoy the view straight across the road to the Royal Mews at the side of Buckingham Palace. On days when the Queen is holding a garden party, you will be able to watch and admire all the fancy frocks and top hats that make their way onto the grounds of the Palace. The 1911 building that houses the Rubens originally was constructed as a residence for debutantes attending parties at Buckingham Palace. During the Second World War, it was used as the headquarters of the Free State Polish Army.

The traditional Afternoon Tea offers sandwiches, scones, and pastries – or you may choose the Devonshire Cream Tea with scones and jam and clotted cream. The hotel's Royal Palace High Tea is not actually a high tea but an afternoon tea with a glass of Joseph Perrier champagne. The tea list includes English Breakfast, Darjeeling, Assam,

"There's a sense of family here, beginning with the portraits on the wall and continuing to the china plates, framed photographs, and gentle lighting. Sink into the rose-colored sofa or one of the elegant armchairs to chat with friends or read a good book."

Sofitel St. James's

Neighborhood: St. James's
6 Waterloo Place, London, SW1Y 4AN

Located just off the Mall, the Sofitel St. James's is housed in a gracious Georgian Grade II listed building that was once the home of Cox's and Kings Bank and now is owned by the Crown Estate. Nearby, you will find St. James's Palace, St. James's Park, the Mall, and Buckingham Palace.

In its conversion from bank to hotel, the building managed to retain many of its classic, historic features, yet lobbies and rooms were updated to have a modern sleek appearance. Visit the Rose Lounge, and you can imagine yourself to be the guest in a comfortable and affluent country house, seated in the drawing room for afternoon tea. There's a sense of family here, beginning with the portraits on the wall and continuing to the china plates and vases in niches and on shelves, framed photographs on the desk, and gentle lighting from cleverly positioned table lamps. Sink into the rose-colored sofa or one of the elegant armchairs with their rose motifs, chat with friends, or read your newspaper or a good book.

With the strains of gentle harp music in the background, you may nibble at finger sandwiches, warm scones, toasted crumpets with oodles of butter, English and French pastries, or a generous slice of one of the homemade cakes that are displayed temptingly on the sideboard. The tea list includes white tea, green tea, Darjeeling, Assam, Ceylon, Earl Grey, Lapsang Souchong, English Breakfast, Orange Blossom, Rose, Jasmine, and a few herbal infusions.

• Afternoon tea served in the Rose Lounge every day, 2:30-5:30pm
• Nearest tube: Charing Cross •
Buses: 6, 9, 15, 23, 139, 176 •
Tel: 020 7747 2205 • Reservations recommended • Major credit cards
• www.sofitel.com • ££

37

Lapsang Souchong, Jasmine, Earl Grey, vanilla, sencha, chocolate, strawberry and mango, and various infusions.

• Afternoon tea served in the Palace Lounge every day, 2:30-5pm • Nearest tube: Victoria • Buses: 2, 36, 185, 436 • Tel: 020 7834 6600 • Reservations recommended • Major credit cards • www.rubenshotel.com • Afternoon Tea, Devonshire Cream Tea, Champagne Tea, Original Crumpet Tea, Royal Palace High Tea, tea by the pot • ££

Shopping Sites for Tea Lovers

Whittard of Chelsea, Buckingham Palace Road
Neighborhood: Victoria
Unit 1, 29 Buckingham Palace Road, London, SW1W 0PP

In the area around Victoria Station, there are two Whittard branches, one in Victoria Place Shopping Centre next to the main railway station and this one opposite the entrance to the Royal Mews at the side of Buckingham Palace. Set in such a popular tourist area, several of the nearby shops offer British souvenirs and memorabilia (just over the road is the Buckingham Palace gift shop selling all sorts of royal souvenirs).

This Whittard shop is light, airy, and painted in pastel shades, with products designed to appeal to foreign visitors – tins shaped as double-decker buses and filled with shortbreads, teapots painted with royal scenes and pictures of the Royal Guardsmen on parade, and mugs decorated with London scenes. The shelves are given over mainly to tea, and you will struggle to find any coffee. Samples are available of the tea of the day.

• Daily 10am-7pm • Nearest tube: Victoria • Buses: 8, 36, 38, 185, 436 • Tel: 020 7821 9698

Whittard of Chelsea, Victoria Station
Neighborhood: Victoria
17a Victoria Place, Victoria Station, London, SW1V 9SJ

• Mon.-Fri. 9am-8pm, Sat. 9am-5pm, and Sun. 9am-3pm • Nearest tube: Victoria • Buses: 36, 185, 436 • Tel: 020 7630 9803

The term Royal Mews hearkens back, not to cats, but to birds. Specifically, falcons. In an earlier day, when falcons were popular pets for royalty and other aristocrats, the regal birds needed special protection while they mewed, or changed their feathers. The area where they were kept during that time became known as the mews. (Source: London Past and Present, *by Henry Wheatley)*

Watch your Language:
English as spoken in London

The United States and England share common roots, but as our histories diverged, so did our language, customs, and traditions. In London, the elevator becomes the *lift*, your tennis shoes become *trainers*, and the bathroom you seek so desperately is, in reality, *the loo*. That waiting line at the tea room is nothing more than a *queue*, and if you want to order the cookies, it'll be wise to call them *biscuits*. When you indulge in tea fare with particular pleasure, you are *tucking into* the food. Here are a few more terms that may be useful as you use this guidebook in London.

Afternoon Tea - No one does afternoon tea like the English. It is a decadent mixture of both sweet and savory tidbits served in high fashion. The usual time for afternoon tea is between 3 and 5 o'clock in the afternoon. Please don't call it *high tea*! High tea (served after 5:30) is a meal with a pot of tea.

Circus – When you arrive at Piccadilly Circus, you'll encounter only the memories of clowns and acrobats, not the real thing. In England, the word *circus* applies to a pattern of streets that roughly form an enclosed circle. Piccadilly Circus is a good example and did indeed have a circular shape until the 1886 construction of Shaftsbury Avenue.

Crumpet – What exactly is this classic British treat? A small, round unsweetened bread cooked on a griddle, toasted and served with butter and jam.

Food hall – England has retained its tradition of large and venerable department stores, including Selfridges, Harrods, and Harvey Nichols. Each has an area set aside to sell upscale food and beverages. Prices tend to be high, but shoppers find unusual products from special suppliers. Some food halls offer light meals and snacks.

Grade II Listed Building - Significant English historic buildings and monuments are the responsibility of English Heritage, a United Kingdom government body with broad authority to manage the historic environment. Buildings are "listed" because of their age, rarity, architectural merit, and method of construction. All buildings built before 1700 that survive in anything like their original condition are listed, as are most built between 1700 and 1840. After that date, the criteria become tighter, so that post-1945 buildings have to be exceptionally important to be listed. Grade I buildings are of exceptional interest; Grade II* are particularly important buildings of more than special interest; Grade II are of special interest, warranting every effort to preserve them.

Market stall - Street markets have always been popular in London, varying widely in their size and range of goods. Food, clothing (new or secondhand), household items, souvenirs, and antiques are available. Every market is divided into stalls, usually containing a basic wooden trestle table and a surrounding frame. Stallholders decorate their space and arrange their goods in an eye-catching fashion. Food stalls usually offer small tasters of their wares, and tea stalls have the varied leaves for shoppers to smell and examine. The markets are ideal for small tea companies with entrepreneurs who are eager to share their knowledge and enthusiasm with shoppers. In this relaxed environment, shoppers find it easy to talk and ask questions.

Tea lounge – In most American cities, a *lounge* is a place that serves cocktails, but Britons have their tea lounges, relaxing areas where patrons may order tea and light fare.

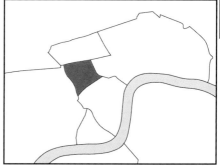

Mayfair and Piccadilly

More than twenty tea lounges and shops open their doors to visitors in this relatively small portion of the city. You'll find British tea traditions here, alongside Japanese and Indian influences that give tea time an Asian twist. The settings offer surprises, too, whether you head into a cafe tucked inside a world-famous auction house or an upscale restaurant set within a massive department store.

Browns Hotel

Neighborhood: Mayfair
Albermarle Street, London, W1S 4BP

While Lord Byron was busy writing timeless poetry such as *Childe Harold* and *Don Juan*, his butler (James Brown) and Lady Byron's maid (Mrs. Brown) were establishing a hotel. They created Browns Hotel in 1837 by purchasing four adjacent houses on Dover Street. Their stated goal was to operate a hotel for the 'gentry and nobility.' Today, Browns still offers the comfort and quality service for which it was originally famous. Best of all, you don't need ties to nobility to enjoy their traditional afternoon tea.

The hotel has been totally refurbished with designs by Olga Polizzi (sister of the current owner, Rocco Forte), and the English Tearoom retains its traditional discreet style but is lighter and brighter than before. The tea selection includes Assam, Darjeeling, Ceylon, China Keemun, Lapsang Souchong, Earl Grey, and English Breakfast. You're free to

Piccadilly Circus (opposite left) is the Times Square of London. It is a roundabout filled with flashing neon signs, congested traffic and wide-eyed tourists. This is the prelude to the theatre district.

choose the one that suits your taste to accompany the Classic Afternoon Tea. The menu includes sandwiches filled with smoked salmon on brown bread, cucumber on caraway bread, honey roast ham with Dijon mustard on poppy seed bread, cheese and tomato on tomato bread, and a little egg and cress bridge roll. Save room for scones plus a selection of pastries and cakes. If you have something special to celebrate, enjoy the bubbly that comes with the Champagne Afternoon Tea.

You don't have to come here just for afternoon tea – the room is open all day, and you may want to drop in for a light lunch or a mid-morning snack. The hotel has added a number of dishes to the menu to satisfy the needs of guests who suffer from food allergies or deal with restrictive diets.

• Brown's English Tearoom open daily, 9am-11pm. Afternoon tea served 3-6pm • Nearest tubes: Green Park, Piccadilly Circus • Buses: 9, 14, 19, 22, 38 • Tel: 020 7493 6020 • Reservations recommended • www.brownshotel.com • Major credit cards • Classic Afternoon Tea, Champagne Afternoon Tea, tea by the pot • £££

Chai Bazaar
Neighborhood: Mayfair
16 Albermarle Street, London W1S 4HW

Take tea at the Chai Bazaar, and you may find yourself sitting regally in an expansive, throne-like, wooden armchair inlaid with mother of pearl, or comfortably ensconced on a soft crimson bench trimmed with silver that was once the headboard of an Indian double bed. The mix-and-match furniture is all pure Indian, and taking tea in this setting makes it easy to imagine that you have been transported to the subcontinent.

This is the only tea room in London serving a variety of excellent quality teas from all the growing regions of India, including Dooars, Terai, Nilgiri, Kashmir, Darjeeling, and Assam. Tea consultant Sanjay Guha spent six months choosing teas and creating blends that suited the local water before the restaurant started serving its Indian afternoon tea. He visits regularly to check that everything is running smoothly, which it always is, thanks to the skills of manager Anshuman Saxena.

Chef Manpreet Ahuja has devised an authentic Indian tea menu of Bombay mix, lightly spiced samosas served with cooling yogurt and tamarind and mint chutney, vegetable pakoras with strawberry chutney, and a tempting selection of miniature sweets. Nibble at cubes of fudge-like barfi, syrup-coated gulabjuman, and Rasmalai made from curd cheese and icing sugar. To cool the mouth, choose green Kashmiri tea poured from a small copper samovar into tiny white

Chai is the Hindi word for tea. Better known as masala chai in India, it is strong black tea enhanced with spices such as cardamom, black pepper, cinnamon, and cloves. It is always served with milk and sugar.

cups containing almond flakes and strands of saffron. Be sure to try one of the four chai masalas served from a traditional *ketley* into glazed earthenware *kulhars*, the smarter version of the tiny throw-away teacups used at roadside tea stalls in India.

• Tea served Mon.-Sat. noon-5:30pm • Nearest tubes: Piccadilly Circus, Green Park • Bus: 9 • Tel: 020 7629 9802 • Reservations accepted • www.chaibazaarindia. com • Major credit cards • Indian-style Afternoon Tea, tea by the pot • £

The Chesterfield
Neighborhood: Mayfair
35 Charles Street, London,
W1J 5EB

Looking for the atmosphere of a comfortable stately home in the English countryside? You may find it in the Conservatory of this bijou Georgian five-star hotel, which is flooded with natural daylight and furnished with a garden theme.

Members of the wait staff, who are especially kind and helpful, will bring your traditional tea on a three-tier cake stand on a trolley. The loose leaf teas include Afternoon Blend, Ceylon, Assam, Darjeeling, Earl Grey, Lapsang Souchong, decaffeinated, Gunpowder, China Oolong, Jasmine, and a few herbal infusions.

The Afternoon Tea consists of finger sandwiches, scones with Devonshire clotted cream and jam, pastries, and fruit cakes. On special occasions, add a little sparkle to your afternoon with the Champagne Afternoon Tea.

For a real indulgence, try the Chocolate Lover's Tea, which brings you hot chocolate or a chocolate milk shake (although they most likely would let you have a pot of tea instead), sandwiches, chocolate scones with clotted cream and jam, and a selection of chocolate pastries, cakes, and a luxury chocolate bar. If you have children with you, this is sure to please.

The Chesterfield is one of several tea venues now including chocolate-themed items on its tea menu. The Chocolate Lover's Tea at this fine hotel features chocolate scones and pastries.

• Afternoon tea served in the Conservatory every day 2:30-5pm • Nearest tube: Green Park • Buses: 36, 436, 16, 148, 414, 73, 2, 82 to Hilton Hotel on Park Lane, then walk • Tel: 020 7491 2622 • Reservations possible but not essential • www.chesterfieldmayfair.com • Major credit cards • Afternoon Tea, Devonshire Cream Tea, Chesterfield Champagne Tea, Chocolate Lover's Tea, tea by the pot • ££

The Connaught Hotel
Neighborhood: Mayfair
Carlos Place, London W1K 2AL

Set close to Grosvenor Square and Berkeley Square, the Connaught is worthy of its prestigious location and has a style that evokes old England. The aptly named Red Room offers an ambience reminiscent of a library or study in a traditional Georgian house. Decorated with black and white prints, this family-size room has a serious air about it and creates a somewhat studious and masculine feel. It's quietly dramatic, too, especially when the tall silver vases are filled with crimson amaryllis to accentuate the rich color of the lounge.

There's more than visual drama here. The tea is very good, and you can enjoy a tasty selection of finger sandwiches including cucumber on rye bread, roasted ham and gruyere cheese, smoked salmon with cream cheese, roast beef with fresh horseradish, and a little egg and cress roll. Add scones with preserves and Cornish clotted cream, toasted crumpets, and pastries, plus your choice of teas. The list includes loose leaf English Breakfast, Earl Grey, Darjeeling, Assam, Lapsang Souchong, China Green, Jasmine, and various herbals. Service here is quiet, courteous, and efficient. You may imagine yourself in your own home, relaxing over a refreshing cup of tea after a busy day.

• Afternoon tea served in the Red Room every day 3-5:30pm • Nearest tubes: Bond Street, Green Park • Buses: 7, 8, 10, 73, 98, 137 to Oxford Street, then walk down Duke Street to Grosvenor Square • Tel: 020 7499 7070 • Reservations recommended • Major credit cards • www.the-connaught.co.uk • Afternoon Tea, Champagne Tea, tea by the pot • ££

Fortnum & Mason St. James's Restaurant
Neighborhood: Piccadilly
181 Piccadilly, London, Tel: 020 7734 8040

As you step out of the lift into the foyer of the tea lounge, expect to see a queue of people waiting patiently for a table in either the lounge or the restaurant. Although St. James's can accommodate many people, it is so popular that guests often encounter a line. Don't worry – the wait will be worth it.

The tables are configured in a very English arrangement of sofas and armchairs, white linen tablecloths, and large paintings of sea and landscapes. Tea is delivered on a three tier cake stand, and you'll dine on the very pretty Fortnum & Mason turquoise china.

Taking tea here offers several choices, including a traditional Afternoon Tea featuring sandwiches with delicious fillings such as chicken with onion marmalade, poached Loch Duart salmon mayonnaise, smoked salmon, crème fraîche and lime, and cream cheese with slivers of cucumber, scones, and pastries.

As tea lovers know, Afternoon Tea was an upper class social gathering at which you could choose whether or not to eat any of the dainty offerings. In contrast, High Tea was developed as a robust working class affair – a family meal that everyone tucked into with great relish. The St. James's knows how to do a proper High Tea. There's Welsh rarebit with sizzling rashers of back bacon, or Scrambling Highlander, Fortnum's famous version of scrambled eggs with smoked salmon on granary toast. Next come the scones with jam and clotted cream, plus various cakes.

Choose your beverage from the Rare Tea Selection (Assam Mohokutie, Darjeeling Chamong, or Darjeeling Jungpana) or the Classic Tea Selection (St. James's Blend, Royal Blend, Queen Anne Blend, Earl Grey Classic, Darjeeling BOP, or Lapsang Souchong). Of course, there is also the option of a Fortnum champagne to go with the food and tea you have chosen. This is a feast guaranteed to fill you up for the rest of the day.

• Closed Sunday. Afternoon tea served in the St. James's Restaurant and Lounge on the Fourth Floor, Mon.-Sat. 3-5:30pm • Nearest tubes: Piccadilly Circus, Green Park • Buses: 9, 14, 19, 22, 38 • Reservations recommended • Major credit cards • www.fortnumandmason.com • Afternoon Tea, High Tea, tea by the pot • £££

Fortnum & Mason Patio Restaurant
181 Piccadilly, London, W1A 1ER

The patio restaurant is situated at the rear of the ground floor of Fortnum's food hall, and you're likely to face a brief queue for a table as it is very popular throughout the day. The teas offered

"Claridges has been famous for its afternoon tea for more than 100 years, and they continue the tradition with a choice of thirty different teas from all over the world. Whatever you sip, it is likely to be a fine accompaniment to the hotel's elegant finger sandwiches."

Claridges

Neighborhood: Mayfair
Brook Street, Mayfair, London, W1A 2JQ

For anyone who loves art deco interiors, Claridges is a must. The entrance is magnificent, and both the Foyer and the Reading Room, where tea is served, are decorated in 1930s style. Fireplaces, leather columns, richly cushioned chairs and banquettes – all of it takes you back to the days of chic geometric designs. At tea-time, everything on the table matches that theme, with Limoges' Galerie Royale porcelain specially created for Claridges, complemented by deco style milk jugs, sugar basins, cake stands, and cutlery. In the background a string quartet plays nostalgic tea-time music, adding to the period feel of the room. This really is an inspirational place in which to take tea.

Claridges has been famous for its afternoon tea for more than one hundred years, and they continue the tradition with a choice of thirty different teas from all over the world including Royal White Silver Needles and Claridges Royal Blend. Whatever you sip, it is likely to be a fine accompaniment to the hotel's elegant finger sandwiches, apple and raisin scones served with Marco Polo Tea-infused jelly and clotted cream, and selected French pastries. The Champagne Afternoon Tea adds a glass of Laurent Perrier champagne, and the exclusive Dom Pérignon Afternoon Tea features that vintage beverage.

• Afternoon tea served in the Foyer and the Reading Room every day, 3-5:30pm • Nearest tube: Bond Street • Buses: 6, 7, 8, 15, 23, 94, 98, 137, 176, 390, then walk down New Bond Street • Tel: 020 7629 8860 • Reservations essential • Major credit cards • www.claridges.co.uk • Afternoon Tea, Champagne Afternoon Tea, Dom Perignon Afternoon Tea, tea by the pot • £££

here are the same as upstairs in the St. James's Restaurant, with the addition of Breakfast Blend, Green Earl Grey, Organic Darjeeling, and several herbal and fruit infusions. The all-day menu includes sumptuous savories such as oysters, lobster in Marie Rose sauce, artichoke pasta, various salads, the famous Fortnum's Welsh rarebit, and wild smoked salmon with sour cream and capers. Sweet treats include carrot cake, Valrhona chocolate and hazelnut torte, Welsh Lady lemon curd sponge, chocolate fondue, tiramisu, crème brûlée, cheesecake, ice cream, and sundaes. Yum! No wonder you have to wait for a table.

The **Fortnum & Mason food hall** has been in the same shop in Piccadilly for 300 years and is a favorite place to shop for high quality teas and groceries. The tea department on the ground floor has grown over the last few years. The range now includes familiar teas from around the world, special Fortnum blends that are featured in the St. James's Restaurant and the Patio Restaurant (Queen Anne, Royal Blend, Irish Breakfast), flavored black and green teas, and a long list of rare and special teas from named estates in India and Sri Lanka (Jade Oolong, Yin Zhen, Rolling Clouds, Jungpana, Margaret's Hope, Okayti, Uva Shawlands), as well as China and Taiwan.

You can also buy Earl Grey, Lapsang Souchong, Fortmason Tea (a blend of teas from India and China flavored with orange blossom), Afternoon Blend, Keemun, Russian Caravan, and Chai. The food hall also carries Green Earl Grey, Green Ceylon, Jasmine, Gunpowder, Moroccan Mint, green with elderflower, green with mango, green with orange, and black teas flavored with strawberry, mango, raspberry, vanilla, bitter orange, and cinnamon.

On the third floor at Fortnum's, you'll find their outstanding antique department with a small but exquisite selection of glass, silver, and porcelain, including beautiful Georgian,

Victorian, and Edwardian teacups, bowls, pots, and jugs. Alongside the antiques, they have modern silver caddy spoons and strainers. Even if you don't intend to buy, it's worth taking a look because of their aesthetic quality and historical value. This shop will tempt you to add to your collection or take a gift home.

• Hours for the Patio Restaurant: Mon.-Sat. 10am-5:30pm, Sun. noon-5pm • Tel: 020 7734 8040 • Major credit cards • ££

• Hours and information for the food hall: Mon.-Sat. 10am-6:30pm, Sun. noon-6pm • Tel: 020 7734 8040 • Major credit cards

Grosvenor House Hotel
Neighborhood: Mayfair
Park Lane, London W1K 7TN

Grosvenor House is a popular, busy hotel, but in the Park Room visitors find a peaceful haven with a view straight out over Park Lane and Hyde Park. This is a generous room of ample proportions and calm atmosphere. The Edwardian style is reflected in the green and gold hues typical of that period, the champagne bar set against the far wall, and the elegance and style with which everything is served.

The tea menu includes all the favorites from times gone by – neat sandwiches, scones with three different jams and clotted cream, followed by traditional chocolate éclairs, meringues, and fruit tarts. All help to recreate memories of times past when children were regularly taken out for tea and expected to behave impeccably.

The Grosvenor House Treat brings you scones with Devonshire clotted cream, fresh mixed berries with vanilla ice cream, and a glass of Piper Heidsieck champagne. On the tea list, you'll find single estate Darjeelings and Assams, along with a Tarry Lapsang Souchong, an English Breakfast Ceylon blend, Queen's tea (a blend of Ceylon and Darjeeling), Earl Grey, Jasmine, Morning Dew (a sencha blended with rose petals, cornflowers, and fruit flavoring), vanilla rooibos, and a few infusions. Each is brewed by a trained tea specialist.

• Afternoon tea served in the Park Room every day, 3-6pm • Nearest tube: Marble Arch • Buses: 36, 436 • Tel: 020 7399 8453 (direct line for Park Room where tea is served) • Reservations recommended • Major credit cards • www.marriott.co.uk • Park Room Afternoon Tea, the Grosvenor House Treat, tea by the pot • ££

H. R. Higgins
Neighborhood: Mayfair
79 Duke Street, London, W1K 5AS

Mr. Higgins established this business in 1942 on South Molton Street and moved to the present location in 1986. Now his son Tony, daughter Audrey, and grandson David run the company,

(continued on page 51)

The Dorchester

Neighborhood: Mayfair
Park Lane, London W1A 2HJ

> "Tea is genteel, unhurried and delicious. But be prepared to make difficult choices, for the tea menu is exceptional."

Enter the Dorchester through the revolving doors just off Park Lane, and you will encounter the grandeur of the Promenade sweeping away to the farthest corner of the hotel. This surely must be one of the longest tea rooms in the world, but don't expect to simply arrive without a booking and find a table. The Dorchester is always busy; make your reservations well in advance.

Once seated, you have the sensation of having arrived in the anteroom of an aristocratic mansion where every item is of the finest quality, members of the staff take care of your every need, and tea is genteel, unhurried and delicious. Be prepared to make difficult choices, for the menu is exceptional. Will you have the impressive Afternoon Tea? It features finger sandwiches filled with cucumber and cream cheese, egg mayonnaise with shiso cress, chicken with mustard mayonnaise, and smoked salmon with cream cheese, scones with strawberry jam and clotted cream, and fantastic little sweet creations. You can add a glass of Rose champagne or a Rossini cocktail if you'd like.

But what about something quite different? The High Tea is ideal if your appetite is good. Make that selection, and you'll have all of the above plus poached eggs Monte Carlo with smoked haddock and champagne froth ... *or* a Cheddar fritter with a mustard sabayon... *or* a salad of breast of chicken and duck liver with New Forest mushrooms and figs. Ah, the choices.

The tea list is even more impressive than the food. You can choose from Dorchester Blend of Silvery Ceylon with Assam, English Breakfast, Assam, Big Red Sun (Kenya and Ceylon), Earl Grey, Darjeeling, and East Frisian Blend (very strong and meant to be drunk with brown sugar and cream). But there's more: Wuyi San Lapsang Souchong, Russian Country, Dragon Pearl Jasmine, Keemun Mao Feng, Chinese Bai Mei, Ceylon Pekoe, and Paris Blend (black tea with fruit, bergamot, and caramel). Need more choices? The tea list includes Bangkok (green tea with lemongrass, ginger, and coconut), Indian Nimbu (lemon and caramel flavored black tea), Vanilla, Ti Kwan Yin Oolong, Sencha, Chamomile, Lemongrass Infusion, African Autumn (Rooibos), strawberry and kiwi infusion, and decaffeinated black tea.

Afternoon tea served in the Promenade every day 2:30-6pm • Nearest tubes: Hyde Park Corner, Green Park, Marble Arch • Buses: 36, 436, 2 • Tel: 020 7629 8888 • Reservations essential • Major credit cards • www.dorchesterhotel.com • Afternoon Tea, Champagne Afternoon Tea, High Tea, tea by the pot • £££

> "Instead of sandwiches, look forward to small tortilla wraps, spring rolls, citrus-cured salmon on a rosemary and caper salad, or prawn remoulade. Those are followed by warm scones and an amazing array of pastries and cakes."

Four Seasons Hotel

Neighborhood: Mayfair
Hamilton Place, Park Lane, W1A 1AZ

Cleverly using its name, the Four Seasons offers a quartet of inventive and delicious seasonal afternoon teas throughout the year as well as a traditional afternoon tea. Instead of sandwiches, look forward to small tortilla wraps, spring rolls, citrus-cured salmon on a rosemary and caper salad, or prawn remoulade. Those are followed by warm scones and an amazing array of pastries and cakes, including hazelnut and raspberry torte, quark cheese and apricot profiteroles, and iced pink champagne mousse with vanilla poached strawberries. For its afternoon tea, the Four Seasons serves salmon, egg and cress, cream cheese and cucumber sandwiches, scones, and pastries. The selections are wonderful and served with impressive attention to detail. You will be offered more of everything at no extra cost, and by the time you have eaten your fill, you will believe yourself in heaven.

Michael Farquhar, lounge manager, takes great pride in the Four Seasons tea experience. Over the past few years, he has developed an excellent list of more than thirty teas from all over the world. Michael knows what his customers enjoy, and he makes sure that there are fine selections to suit all tastes. You may choose from excellent Darjeelings and Assams, or try the Japanese Sencha, Rose Pouchong, Keemun, Pai Mu Tan, the Queen Mary Blend, or the Anniversary Blend. Michael's staff members are extremely well trained, not only in their knowledge of tea but also in their gracious and charming approach to serving guests. The resident pianist happily entertains everyone with medleys of favorite songs and show tunes. In this calm Edwardian-style room, it is impossible not to have a truly wonderful time.

• Afternoon tea served every day, 3-7pm • Nearest tubes: Green Park, Hyde Par Corner • Buses: 8, 9, 14, 19, 22, 36, 38, 436 • Tel: 020 7499 0888 • Reservations recommended • Major credit cards • www.fourseasons.com/london • Five-star hotel serving afternoon tea, seasonal teas, tea by the pot • £££

with Tony's wife, Jean Mavis, organizing the presentation of goods and wares. They all strive to continue the family tradition of personal service and high quality products. Customers all over Britain have been buying quality teas and coffees from them for years.

The shop itself has a lovely old-fashioned charm and elegance. In the front window, you'll see old coffee-making equipment. Step inside, and you'll find an interior that is both inviting and efficient with its wooden counter, old brass weighing scales, japanned tins filled with loose teas, and neat brown paper packaging. A special counter displays teapots, infusers, brewing mugs, and caddies.

Downstairs in the small coffee and tea room, customers take a short break from shopping or business to enjoy one of the excellent teas. You can try the strong, full-flavored Duke Street Blend or the Higgins Afternoon Blend that mixes China and Indian black teas. The Higgins Breakfast Blend is created from Ceylon, India, and Kenya teas, and Higgins Country House Blend of China, Indian and Ceylon teas gives an aromatic, delicate, smooth tea.

There is also Lapsang Souchong, Russian Caravan, Earl Grey, Blue Lady, Yunnan, black teas flavored with apple, lemon, or mango, four seasonal teas, Jasmine, Lung Ching, Oolong, Rose Congou, single estate Assams, Darjeelings, and a Sikkim from Temi plantation. After a refreshing pot of tea, it's easy to walk back up to Oxford Street and continue shopping.

• Mon.-Fri. 9:30am-5:30pm, Sat. 10am-5pm • Nearest tube: Bond Street • Buses: 7, 8, 10, 73, 98, 137 to Oxford Street, then walk down Duke Street • Tel: 020 7629 3913 or 020 7491 8819 • Retail shop selling loose teas and coffees, small coffee bar serving tea and coffee • www.hrhiggins. co.uk • Major credit cards • via e-mail: orders@ hrhiggins.co.uk • £

Le Meridien Piccadilly Hotel
Neighborhood: Piccadilly
21 Piccadilly, London, W1J 0BH

Tea at Le Meridien Piccadilly used to be taken in the Oak Room Lounge on the ground floor, and you still may still find it served there on special occasions. However, the Terrace Restaurant on the second floor is now the typical venue for an afternoon indulgence. Take the lift to the restaurant, turn left and enter the stone-clad lobby of the airy, conservatory room. The neutral colors of the walls and floor are an excellent foil for the extremely bright and very large abstract paintings that decorate the walls. More color is added by the dramatic tropical flowers that sit in vases on each table.

On the list of teas are a few unusual blends such as Marco Polo (a Chinese tea mixed with Oriental flowers and fruits), Thé Sur le Nil (citrus

51

The Terrace Restaurant at Le Meridien Piccadilly makes tea feel like an afternoon indulgence, complete with background music from the resident pianist and views out over Piccadilly's busy shopping street.

flavored), and Earl Grey Imperial (a bergamot flavored Darjeeling), as well as First, Second, and Autumnal Darjeelings, English Breakfast, Lapsang Souchong, and Jasmine. Afternoon Tea includes all the traditional elements, while the Terrace Champagne Tea adds smoked fish and caviar with blinis and a glass of champagne. Terrace Cheese Tea brings you a platter of traditional English cheeses with Port, homemade scones, and clotted cream and strawberry jam. Enjoy this along with music from the resident pianist and views out over Piccadilly's busy shopping street.

• Afternoon tea served in the Terrace Restaurant every day, 3-6pm • Nearest tube: Piccadilly Circus • Buses: 9, 14, 19, 22, 38 • Tel: 020 7734 8000 • Reservations recommended but not essential • Major credit cards • www.lemeridien. com • Afternoon Tea, Terrace Cheese Tea, Terrace Champagne Tea, Tea by the pot • £££

Momo
Neighborhood: West End
23-25 Heddon Street, London, W1B 4BH

Momo is situated in a quiet cul-de-sac off Regent Street, at one time an unremarkable section of London but now a thriving area marked by a good selection of trendy restaurants. Outside Momo, the pavement is decorated to resemble the entrance to a Moroccan souk, with colorful rugs laid out and soft leather stools set around low round brass tables. As you walk inside, heady wafts of perfumed incense greet you.

This is not your ordinary restaurant. North African lamps hang from the ceiling, and small niches in the walls are filled with carvings, goblets, boxes, jewellery, vases, and books. In one corner, a rail holds Moroccan clothing that is for sale. The bar, set against one wall, is decked with teapots – and hookahs, too, for people who come to sociably smoke fruit-flavored or sheesha tobacco with friends. The mood of the room is set by the earthy tones that surround you. Cushions, benches, floor tiles, and walls reflect rich colors of clay and wood, brightened by traditional Arabic patterns and inlaid shell and mother-of-pearl set into the table tops. Carefully selected African and Latin American music adds to the charm. Momo has an atmosphere that encourages guests to return again and again.

The cardamom tea is a personal favorite, but you may choose mint, mint with orange blossom, pine nuts or rose water, jasmine, Earl Grey, green tea, mint tea with cinnamon, chamomile, lemon and ginger, or orange mango and cinnamon. All teas are brewed in elegant Moroccan silver pots and delivered to the table with tea glasses stacked and upturned onto the spout. Handsome waiters and beautiful waitresses pour a clear stream of tea from a height of about ten inches, sending it cleanly into the little glasses. They leave you to sip and soak up the intriguing atmosphere.

You may also want something to eat, so order kofta or grilled chicken wraps, a vegetarian salad, or lamb kebab. For something sweet, try the almond pistachio moelleux or the Maghrebi pastries.

• Daily noon-1am • Nearest tubes: Piccadilly Circus, Oxford Circus • Buses: 6, 9, 15, 23 to Piccadilly Circus then walk up Regent Street • Tel: 020 7434 4040 • Moroccan restaurant, Kemia Bar, Tea Room and Bazaar serving tea, food, wines • Major credit cards • Tea by the pot • ££

Park Lane Hotel
Neighborhood: Piccadilly
Piccadilly, London, W1J 7BX

If the ballroom in the Park Lane Hotel seems familiar, there could be a reason. It has provided the location for several films and television dramas (*Brideshead Revisited, Shanghai Surprise, Jeeves and Wooster, Mona Lisa*). Built between 1924 and 1927, the hotel has retained many of its art deco

53

features. Tea is served in the Palm Court, and as you walk through the swing doors, look to the walls behind you to admire the original art deco sunburst mirrors.

The subdued lighting is very soothing, and as your eyes become accustomed, you will notice that the fabrics used throughout the room have a wonderfully subtle golden sheen. The gilded effect is reflected in the painted ceiling. Along the walls are chinoiserie panels and large palms that create an exotic period atmosphere. The low tables are covered with pure white linen cloths and set with fine white china trimmed in black and gold.

You can order something simple and spare to eat accompanied by a pot of tea (Assam, Ceylon, Darjeeling, Earl Grey, English Breakfast, Gunpowder, Jasmine, Formosa Oolong, Keemun, Yunnan, Lady Grey, Russian Caravan, Prince of Wales Tea, Queen Mary Blend, Pear and Vanilla). Or you can indulge in the full Afternoon Tea with all the usual treats or perhaps the Art Deco Tea with a glass of champagne. Another option is the Pear and Vanilla Tea, complete with a glass of vanilla flavored champagne, sandwiches, scones, and a selection of pastries all flavored with pear and vanilla. But the most distinctive set tea is the Pink Tea with its pink champagne, rose flavored tea, pink pastries, a pink shot glass (a pink mousse or jelly or something luxuriously similar), and a gift for each female member of the group. With this tea, any day can be Valentine's Day. It is well worth going out to tea.

• Afternoon tea served in the Palm Court every day, 3-5pm • Nearest tubes: Hyde Park Corner, Green Park • Buses: 19, 22, 38 • Telephone: 020 7499 6321 • Reservations recommended • www.starwoodhotels.com • Major credit cards • Afternoon Tea, Pink Afternoon Tea, Art Deco Tea, Pear and Vanilla Tea, tea by the pot • ££

The Ritz

Neighborhood: Piccadilly
150 Piccadilly, London, W1J 9BR

How good is tea at the Ritz? Well, you have to make reservations at least six weeks in advance. And it's still the kind of place where gentlemen must wear a jacket and tie. The hotel is prepared to lend something suitable to a guest who arrives unaware, but jeans and trainers (tennis shoes) are forbidden. Do dress up and enjoy a little glamour.

Tea at the Ritz has a ring to it that tempts people from all over the world. This is probably the busiest and most popular venue in London, and it is absolutely essential to book in advance. What-

The Ritz is probably the busiest and most popular tea venue in London, and it is absolutely essential to book in advance.

ever time you decide to visit, you are bound to enjoy yourself. The setting is stylish, sophisticated, and elegant, with gilded furniture, fine porcelain, crisp tablecloths, linen napkins, excellent service, delicious food, and very good tea. It is expensive, but you can eat as much as you want, and you will be well looked after.

Make your selection of either the Afternoon Tea or the Champagne Tea, then settle on a particular pot of tea. You can choose from the Ritz Royal English (a blend of Assam, Ceylon and Kenya), Darjeeling First Flush, Tippy Assam, Ceylon Orange Pekoe, Russian Caravan, Earl Grey, Lapsang Souchong Imperial, Jasmine with flowers, Rose Congou, Chun Mee, Formosa Oolong, and infusions.

The food is excellent – sandwiches on a selection of different breads filled with smoked salmon, ham, chicken mayonnaise, and cucumber and cream cheese. The raisin and apple scones are served with clotted cream and organic strawberry preserves, the cakes and pastries are irresistible, and then - just in case you haven't yet eaten enough - comes a compote of fruits of the forest bathed in English cream. A veritable feast.

• Afternoon tea served every day at 11:30am, 1:30pm, 3:30pm, 5:30pm, and 7:30pm • Nearest tubes: Green Park, Piccadilly Circus • Buses: 9, 14, 19, 22, 38 • Tel: 020 7493 8181 • Reservations essential, at least six weeks ahead; book by telephone or online • Major credit cards • www.theritzlondon.com • Afternoon Tea, Champagne Tea • £££

Sotheby's Cafe
Neighborhood: Mayfair
34-35 New Bond Street, London, W1A 2AA

Sotheby's is world famous for its elegant auctions, with bidders willing to pay seven-figure sums for fine art and historical treasures. But there's no need to bid if you simply want fine tea in a fine art setting. Sotheby's Cafe is open to the public and offers pleasant surroundings where you can watch stylish people come and go in the auction house.

The cafe at Sotheby's offers fine tea in a fine art setting, where patrons can watch stylish people come and go in the auction house.

The small cafe spills out into the foyer, so you can sit peacefully at your table but still feel part of the daily activity. On the walls of the cafe (and in corridors and the ladies' loo), there are entrancing black and white photos of great stars and literary figures. The tables are dressed in white linen, and the mood is comfortable but sophisticated.

Food here is designed to please the eye as well as the palate. During the day, there are light snacks and lunchtime dishes, and at tea-time the menu offers beautiful open sandwiches, scones, and extremely pretty tartlets and cakes. Instead, you may choose Sotheby's Small Tea of toasted teacakes with orange and cinnamon butter (a lovely twist on an old favorite) or scones with clotted cream and damson jam (so nice to have a change from strawberry). You could opt for the high tea savories-Welsh rarebit or smoked salmon with brown bread and butter. Sweet treats include marble cake and lemon cake. The list of loose teas includes Breakfast Blend, Sotheby's House Blend, Darjeeling, Lapsang Souchong, Oolong, Ceylon Pekoe, Earl Grey, and herbal infusions.

• Sotheby's Cafe open Mon.-Fri. 9:30am-5pm, Afternoon Tea served 3-4:45pm • Nearest tubes: Bond Street, Oxford Circus • Buses: 6, 7, 8, 15, 23, 94, 98, 137, 390 to Oxford Street, then walk down New Bond Street • Tel: 020 7293 5077 • Reservations highly recommended • Major credit cards • Afternoon Tea, Sotheby's Small Tea, tea by the pot • £

The Wolseley
Neighborhood: Piccadilly
160 Piccadilly, London, W1J 9EB

This stunning building with its ornate interior was commissioned by the Wolseley car company in 1921 as its London showroom. In 1929, it became a bank and, later, a Chinese restaurant and tea house. The black lacquer work around the room was changed to Chinese imperial red, but its time here was limited. In 2003, the building reopened as the Wolseley. Now black and gold again, it houses a splendid, all-day dining haven

"A great deal of thought has gone into this perfect little shop to create an atmosphere that is a blend of tea, art, history, and life as it should be lived."

Postcard Teas

Neighborhood: Mayfair
9 Dering Street, London, W1AG

Tim d'Offay is co-owner of East Teas, which has a stall in Borough Market, and this exquisite jewel of a shop is Tim's new venture on his own. When he was a boy, he lived in this building on Dering Street, and at one time his father ran it as a prime London art gallery.

Tim's background is in Oriental religions, and while travelling in Japan and Taiwan, he discovered and fell in love with teas from the parts of the world he had studied. He has also, for a long time, collected postcards with tea themes, including pictures of plantations, pickers, and tea advertisements. His collection now numbers more than five hundred postcards that range from quirky to charming. The shop at Nine Dering Street combines a display of his postcards with the teas he loves.

You will find a range of Postcard Teas, which include First Flush, Second Flush, Monsoon, Autumnal and Oolong tea from Ashok Kumar's Goomtee Estate in Darjeeling, Mangalam Estate in Assam, and Handunugoda Estate in Sri Lanka's Galle district. East Teas products are represented with selections from Japan, China, Korea, and Taiwan.

Every tea that Tim sells represents a connection with a tea estate where he knows the planters and pickers. Currently he is working with Handunugoda Estate in Sri Lanka to develop flavored teas using the cinnamon, ginger, cloves, and vanilla grown on the estate. Tim donates a portion of his profits back to the estates to help buy boats and outboard motors for the villagers.

The shop carries all the accessories needed to brew and serve tea plus a range of tea-related postcards. At a long narrow table, paired with neat square stools covered in Indian fabric, customers may try any teas on offer before making a purchase. The leaves are brewed in the pantry, then decanted into a cup and brought to the table. If you decide to buy a packet or tin of the sampled tea, you will not be charged for the cup you drank. The food to go with the infusions is simple, homely, and unfussy – delicious cakes, nuts, dried fruit, and other nibbly things.

In the gallery, Tim's father runs exhibitions of postcards and postcard history. A great deal of thought has gone into this perfect little shop to create an atmosphere that is a blend of tea, art, history, and life as it should be lived.

• Tea tasting room and retail shop open Tue.-Sat., 10:30am-6:30pm • Nearest tube: Bond Street • Buses: 6, 7, 8, 15, 23, 94, 98, 137, 176, 390 then walk down New Bond Street • Tel: 020 7629 3654 • www.postcardteas.com • Major credit cards • £

and is much loved by Londoners and visitors alike.

The clever menu manages to offer exactly what you fancy, no matter what time of day or evening. It's a pleasure to meet friends here for Sunday brunch, a drink in the evening, or a snack after the theatre. When you arrive you are greeted as if you are the most important guest of the day (and they will remember you when you visit again), and a table will be found for you as quickly as possible.

At tea time, choose the Wolseley Blend or English Breakfast, Earl Grey, Darjeeling, Jasmine, Assam, Lapsang Souchong, green, or decaffeinated. The sandwiches with the set tea include cream cheese and celery (nice for a change instead of cucumber), smoked salmon, roasted chicken, egg mayonnaise, and cucumber. The jam is homemade, the scones light and delicious, and the pastries lovely. Tea here is a treat.

• Mon.-Fri. 7am-midnight, Sat. 9am-midnight, Sun. 9am-11pm. Afternoon Tea served Mon.-Fri. 3-5:30pm, Sat.-Sun. 3:30-6pm • www.thewolseley.com • Major credit cards • Nearest tubes: Green Park, Piccadilly Circus • Buses: 9, 22, 38 • Tel: 020 7499 6996 • Reservations recommended • Afternoon Tea, Cream Tea, tea à la carte, tea by the pot • ££

A Royal Warrant, such as the one held by Aspreys, is a grant made by a member of the British Royal Family to a company or person who supplies goods or services to the royal family. The warrant allows the business to advertise the relationship, lending a unique cachet.

By Appointment to Her Majesty The Queen

Shopping Sites for Tea Lovers

Aspreys
Neighborhood: Mayfair
165-168 New Bond Street, London W1S 4AY

Aspreys' beautiful Georgian building dates from the 1790s and has quite a history of illustrious clients. Kings, queens, princes, and princesses from Europe and India have glided through the stately curved glass doors that lead into the shop from New Bond Street. The store still holds three royal warrants – to HM the Queen, the late Queen Mother, and HRH the Prince of Wales.

"Sketch has a well deserved reputation as the most exotic and luxurious tea venue in London, marked by quirky decor, an eclectic tea list, artistically mouth-watering patisseries, and celebrity clientele."

Sketch

Neighborhood: Mayfair
9 Conduit Street, Mayfair, London, W1S 2XG

Sketch has a well deserved reputation as the most exotic and luxurious tea venue in London, marked by quirky decor, an eclectic tea list, artistically mouth-watering patisseries, and celebrity clientele. Even the entrance piques a sense of fascination with the unknown. The stone floor has a childhood hop-scotch game marked out on the flagstones, slightly surreal benches and tables emerge from and merge with the plaster of the walls, and an arched ceiling shimmers in bronze. At the far end of the entrance, you see a dark cavern with a flashing neon light and a figure who sits guarding the entrance to the upper Lecture Room and Gallery Restaurant.

Enough to capture anyone's interest, but stay on the ground floor and turn right into the Parlour, absorbing the fantasy of colors, shapes, and mirrors. The ceiling in half the room is patterned with bright red circles, while the other half sports black and red lines. Chairs and sofas range from red plush to deep sienna, black and white check, or red leather with black lacquer and gilded frames. A stark white counter displays teapots, cups, and saucers ready for service to the tables.

Tiny cake stands and chilled cabinets display cakes that no visitor can long resist. Try the Gui Hong, choux pastry with milk chocolate and Gui-Hong tea cream, or the Latour marzipan chocolate cake with coconut and praline mousse. There's Florence shortbread paste with rhubarb and rosemary marmalade, almond mousse and orange blossom glaze, and Cardinal blackcurrant macaroon with blackcurrant marmalade and violet mousseline cream. Several soft sweet indulgences come in a glass – strawberry compote with vanilla panna cotta, or Campari cherries with chocolate mousse and Amandel chocolate.

If you prefer something savory, you'll find sandwiches filled with ham and Meaux mustard, or piquillos, tomato, courgette and aubergine or smoked salmon, cucumber, dill and cream. The rare teas include Chinese White Jasmine, Iron Goddess oolong, Longjing, Sencha Lemon Sunrise, single estate Darjeeling, Assam and Ceylon, chai, and a selection of Ayurvedic infusions, all of which are brewed in the pantry area using infuser baskets and timers so that each pot is perfect.

• Afternoon tea served in the Parlour Mon.-Sat. 3-6:30pm. Also open for breakfast, lunch, tea, and snacks Mon.-Fri. 8am-11pm, Sat. 10am-11:15pm • Nearest tubes: Bond Street, Oxford Circus • Buses: 6, 7, 8, 15, 23, 94, 98, 137, 176, 390 then walk down New Bond Street • Tel: 0870 777 4488 • Reservations recommended • Major credit cards • www.sketch.uk.com • ££

The shop is an amazing fusion of graciously old and stylishly modern, with a magnificent swirling staircase by Norman Foster leading up from the main floor. Browse around this historical store and you are bound to be tempted. Tea wares are displayed in elegant grandeur on the mezzanine level at the back of the shop, and here you will find the Grafton range of pure white porcelain teapots, cups, and saucers trimmed with platinum trim, the Botanical range decorated with flowers taken from some rediscovered 1790 drawings, and silver teapots, milk jugs, sugar bowls, trays, and teaspoons in several designs, including one in a stunning art deco style.

Set high on a glass shelf behind the counter is a giant Grafton teapot large enough to fill at least 100 teacups (price £3100!). It appears rather too heavy to use for hot tea, but on a summer tea table, it would make an ideal centrepiece, filled with iced tea served with a silver ladle.

• Mon.-Sat. 10am-6pm • Nearest tube: Bond Street, Oxford Circus • Bus: 9, 14, 19, 23, 38, 22 to the Royal Academy and then walk up Bond Street, or 23, 19, 38, 22 to Oxford Circus and walk along Oxford Street and down New Bond Street • Tel: 020 7493 6767 • Silver and porcelain retailers by appointment to Her Majesty the Queen • Major credit cards • www.aspreys.com • Porcelain and silver teapots, teaspoons, other table wares

Genmaicha is Sencha green tea combined with roasted and popped brown rice. This unique combination of flavors may be the most popular Japanese tea outside of Tokyo.

Minamoto Kitchoan
Neighborhood: Piccadilly
44 Piccadilly, London W1J 0DS

Minamoto Kitchoan translates roughly as 'fast meeting place where you will find happiness,' and if you like Japanese sweets and Japanese style, this shop will enchant you. Set in a very British part of London, the shop is unexpected, yet strangely at home amongst its grand neighbors. It offers traditional Japanese sweets and a small range of Japanese green teas (Karigana, Genmaicha, Sencha, and Matcha) in divine packaging. The window display changes according to the season. You may find a charming scene created with dolls or an educational presentation about the Japanese Green Tea Ceremony, complete with traditional kimonos and the necessary tea equipage.

Inside, the decor is totally Japanese with a counter of black lacquer and glass that sweeps the length of the shop. Don't miss the ancient screen from the middle of the Edo period, Japanese calligraphy, lacquer trays and dishes that display sweets and, near the door, a dainty black table and little red stools where customers can perch to eat their favorite *wagashi*.

You'll be tempted by Tuyu, made from sweet red bean paste sandwiched between mini sweet pancakes; Kuzumanju, mild sweet red bean paste wrapped in green tea jelly; or Tsuyaguri, a whole chestnut wrapped in mashed chestnut puree. There are so many of these beautifully presented sweets that you will need time to gaze and admire, question, and consider before deciding.

• Sun.-Fri. 10am-7pm, Sat. 10am-8pm • Nearest tube: Piccadilly Circus • Buses: 9, 14, 19, 22, 38 • Tel: 020 7437 3135 • Retail store selling Japanese tea and sweets to serve with tea • Major credit cards • www.kitchoan.com

Thomas Goode
Neighborhood: Mayfair
19 So. Audley St., Mayfair, London, W1K 2BN

Walk through the quirky, mechanical self-opening door of this fabulous shop (dating back to 1827), and you will feel like a child who has been given too many wonderfully pretty things with which to play. It's hard to know what to enjoy first. The shop is made up of many rooms, each leading into another in an intriguing way and all filled with dazzlingly beautiful things. The selection of tea wares will suit all tastes – classic, modern, period, eccentric, simple, colorful, and starkly plain. There are pots, cups and saucers; tea sets for two with their own porcelain tray; and silver tea knives, pastry forks, cake slicers, teaspoons, and place markers.

In a treasure room at the back, you will find antique silver cake stands, baskets, tea knives and forks, strainers, jugs, basins, trays, and everything you could possibly need for afternoon tea. The linen department has napkins and tablecloths, and there are candles that would make the plainest tea table quite stunning. The museum holds a fine collection of designs and plates representing

One step into Thomas Goode (through a quirky self-opening door), and visitors sense the quality that has marked this business since it opened in 1827.

the work of the company through the years. Even if you are determined to simply browse, do visit this shop. It's a beautiful Georgian building filled with beautiful things.

• Mon.-Sat, 10am-6pm • Nearest tubes: Hyde Park Corner, Green Park, Bond Street • Buses: 36, 436 to London Hilton, then walk • Tel: 020 7499 2823 • www.thomasgoode.co.uk • Retail shop selling very fine porcelain, silver, linens • Major credit cards

Yumchaa, St. James's Market
Neighborhood: Piccadilly
St. James's Church Court Yard
Piccadilly, London, W1

This market stall sells many of the loose leaf teas and infusions so popular at the main Yumchaa shop located at the Camden Lock Market. Run by a group of dynamic young people, Yumchaa is marked by a strong desire to teach people about tea. Yumchaa has other locations on Portobello Road and at the Leadenhall Market. See details in the Camden Lock Market listing.

• Open Fri. 10:45am-6pm, Sat. 9am-6pm • Nearest tube: Piccadilly • Buses: 3, 9, 12, 14, 19, 22, 38, 453

Along Piccadilly, the arcades offer a great opportunity to window shop as you stroll. You may pop into the Waterford shop for a crystal souvenir after having tea at the Ritz or the Woseley.

Harrow-on-the-Hill and Other Mystic Places: The stories behind the names

For those new to England, the place names in a guidebook may sound musical and mysterious: Marylebone, Battersea, Harrow-on-the-Hill. It's clear you're not in Kansas - nor Brooklyn, Los Angeles, or Wyoming.

In every nation, place names carry stories of native peoples, invaders, and years of adaptation for words and phrases. The barest glance at an atlas of the United States reveals a melange of names derived from Native Americans (Dakota, Mississippi, Tennessee) and the subsequent influx of European settlers, including Dutch (Brooklyn), English (Jamestown) French (St. Louis), and Spanish (Las Vegas). Contrast this to English names, which are rooted in Celtic, Saxon, and the language brought by Roman soldiers. Christianity heavily influenced British names, too, because England's period of greatest growth coincided with an era when the Church of England dominated public life. Consider a few stories that explain the names of uniquely British places.

Battersea - A curious corruption of an old name, *Patricsey*, a Saxon phrase for *Peter's river or water*.

Marylebone (*pronounced marra-ly-bone*) - A shortened, smoothed version of St.-Mary's-on-le-bourne, denoting a church beside a small creek.

Harrow-on-the-Hill - Possibly a reference to an ancient Celtic temple (*harrow*) that held a place of prominence.

The Bentley, The Chesterfield, The Lanesborough - The very British use of *The* in a business name hints at exclusivity in a manner reminiscent of royalty and aristocracy.

St. James's Market, St. Paul's Cathedral, St. Martin's Lane - The number of places named for saints reflects the central role of the church in British history in the past millennia. Most frequently referenced saints? James, the beloved disciple, and Mary, the mother of Jesus.

Shad Thames - A corruption of St. John at Thames, referring to Knights Templar who once controlled the area. (Don't forget that London's famous river is pronounced as if the spelling were *Tems*.)

For more information on British history and place names, consult *London: Past and Present* (Henry Wheatley, 1891; reissued by Singing Tree Press).

The name **Blackfriars** was first used in 1342 and derives from the black habits of the Dominican Friars who moved their priory from Holborn to the area between the River Thames and Ludgate Hill in 1276. The priory was eventually closed in 1538 during Henry's dissolution of the monasteries. Some of the buildings were leased to entrepreneurs who started the Blackfriars Theatre, not far from the Globe Theatre.

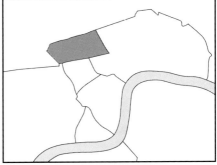

West End
and Marylebone

London's West End offers residents and
tourists alike a vast range of department
stores and fashion shops, street markets
and places of interest such as the Wallace
Collection, Madame Tussaud's, and
Regents Park. Here you can
mix culture with history, and
tea drinking with shopping.

Hyatt Regency London, the Churchill
Neighborhood: West End
30 Portman Square, London W1A 4ZX

When you have finished shopping in Selfridges
or John Lewis (favorite stores on Oxford Street),
walk around the corner to Portman Square, step to
your left through the marble lined lobby, and take
tea in the Montagu lounge. The room is decorated
in calm neutral grays and browns, and concealed
lighting in the gently curved ceiling casts a soft,
warm glow. You could sit here quite comfortably
for an hour or so and take tea.

Enjoy the full Montagu Afternoon Tea with finger
sandwiches, scones with strawberry jam and
Cornish clotted cream, fruit tartlets, and pastries,
or choose the special Churchill Tea with a glass
of Pol Roger Champagne (Sir Winston's favorite).
The teas include the Montagu Blend, English
Breakfast, Earl Grey, Keemun, Darjeeling, Lapsang
Souchong, Jasmine, Japanese Sencha Fukujyu,

*Marylebone
Station, with its
red brick turrets
(opposite),
has become
immortalized
as one of the
stations found
on the British
Monopoly
gameboard.*

and various herbal infusions. All are brewed in pretty white porcelain pots.

• Afternoon tea served in the Montagu every day, 3-6pm.• Nearest tubes: Bond Street, Marble Arch • Buses: 36 to Marble Arch and walk, 2 to Gloucester Place and walk, or 10, 113, 137, 189, 189 to Oxford Street and walk • Tel: 020 7486 5800 • Reservations recommended • Major credit cards • www.london.churchill.hyatt.com • Montagu Afternoon Tea, Churchill Tea, tea by the pot • ££

Landmark Hotel
Neighborhood: Marylebone
222 Marylebone Road, London, NW1 6TQ

The Landmark Hotel is the old Marylebone station hotel and adjoins the railway station at the back; many features of the Victorian building remain. The entrance is stately, the furnishings have an understated elegance, and the atrium in the Winter Garden features high ceilings. The space to the glass dome stretches up at least seven floors and creates a wonderful sense of natural light and space. Palm trees, orchids, and exotic flowers add their foliage and color to the illusion. Stonework that is part of the lounge area reinforces the uncluttered, spacious feel of the room, and guests sit relaxed for hours sipping tea, chatting quietly, and enjoying the calm and peaceful atmosphere.

Choose from a long list of loose leaf teas: Gunpowder green, Lapsang Souchong, Assam, Darjeeling, English Breakfast, Russian Caravan, Earl Grey, Earl Grey Blue Flower, Jasmine, spice flavored, vanilla flavored, and several herbal and mixed-fruit infusions. The set tea brings traditional sandwiches, buttered tea breads, scones, and French pastries, while the Landmark Tea adds strawberries and cream, plus a glass of Taittinger Reserve Brut champagne. You can also have simply a selection of pastries and a pot of tea.

• Afternoon tea served every day, 3-6pm • Nearest tube: Marylebone, Baker Street • Tel: 020 7631 8000 • Five-star hotel serving afternoon tea • Reservations recommended but not essential • Major credit cards • www.landmarklondon. co.uk • Afternoon Tea, Landmark Tea, tea by the pot • ££

The Sanderson

Neighborhood: West End
50 Berners Street, London W1T 3NG

Like its sister hotel, St. Martin's Lane, Sanderson's style and decor are highly original, eccentric, and quirky. As you walk into the lobby, you will be struck by the vast open space of the entire ground floor. The space is put to good advantage with an oversize gilded sofa draped with fur, seats swinging from the ceiling, and African carved stools and chairs. Look, too, for the Venetian glass, mirrors, and chandeliers, Dali's famous Mae West lips sofa, tiny spindle-legged tables, and large outsize cupboards. It's another version of Alice through the Looking Glass and into Wonderland.

St. Marylebone Parish Church was built in 1817, and one of its first organists was Charles Wesley.

For tea, make your way to the Courtyard Restaurant, an outdoor haven with water, trees, and box bushes growing in silver tubs, complete with overhead heaters for cooler weather and chunky rustic furniture. Or visit Spoon, the stylish restaurant. Here you may want to try the set tea known as TeaSpoon, consisting of pastrami and smoked salmon sandwiches, plus the chef's selection of cakes and pastries. Instead, you may want to choose from the menu and have a pot of tea with scones, clotted cream and red fruit compote, along with Spoon Dessert (a sampling of four delicious sweet treats to share around the table) or Top Dessert (four of the best cakes and puddings for sharing), or homemade cookies. As at St. Martins, the teas (Darjeeling, Green, English Breakfast, Earl Grey, chamomile, and peppermint) are all organic and bagged.

• Afternoon tea served in Spoon and in the Courtyard Restaurant every day, 3-4:45pm; 24 hours notice needed for full afternoon tea • Nearest tube: Tottenham Court Road, Oxford Circus • Buses: 7, 8, 10, 25, 55, 73, 98, 176 • Tel: 020 7300 1400 • Reservations not necessary • Major credit cards • www.sandersonlondon.com • TeaSpoon Afternoon Tea, Afternoon Tea à la carte, tea by the pot • ££

Shopping Sites for Tea Lovers

Emma Bridgewater

Neighborhood: Marylebone
81a Marylebone High Street, London, W1U 4QL

The shapes and patterns of Emma Bridgewater's designs are very distinctive, and many British homes have a teapot or a few mugs, porridge bowls, cups, and saucers from this very popular pottery. The designs (all on a pale cream or white background) are bold, graphic, and fun. You can buy teapots covered with pink hearts, green clover leaves, multi-colored polka dots, bright red tulips, roses, or bold black lettering saying chirpy things such as 'Rise and Shine' or 'I love you more than

THOMAS LORD
laid out his original
CRICKET GROUND
on this site in 1787.
The M.C.C. was founded
here in the same year.

Small historical markers are scattered throughout London, often marking the former homes of famous people.

chocolate.' Every teapot is large, generous, practical, sturdy, and chummy – perfect for a leisurely breakfast or a family tea around the kitchen table. Any item would make an excellent gift. (Second Emma Bridgewater location in West London on Fulham Road.)

• Sun. 11am-4pm, Mon.-Sat. 10am-6pm, open until 7 pm on Thur. • Nearest tubes: Bond Street, Regents Park • Buses: 18, 309, 205 to York Gate, then walk down Marylebone High Street • Tel: 020 7486 6897 • Major credit cards • www.emmabridgewater.co.uk • Retail store selling pottery tea wares

Selfridges Food Hall
Neighborhood: West End
400 Oxford Street, London, W1A 1AB

The food hall is a delightful feature of upscale British department stores – a food boutique filled with hard-to-find culinary treasures. The food hall at Selfridges is especially comprehensive, selling take-away and ready-to-eat items, fresh vegetables, meat, fish, cakes and pastries, chocolates, and groceries. Given the limited space in this area of the store, the tea shelves manage to offer a good selection of loose and bagged teas including some rare and innovative types.

You will find Ceylon teas from Dilmah and pyramid teabags of oolong, decaffeinated, white, and English Breakfast in silver triangular tins from

an American company called Revolution. Also at hand are Brewhaha teabags, Ayurvedic teas from Higher Living, loose teas from Williamson and Magor in their elephant-shaped tins, and selections from the Yorkshire company, Taylors of Harrogate. Selfridges stocks organic and fair trade teas from Hampstead Tea and Coffee, plus a range of herbal and fruit infusions. Look for special items from the Hong Kong company, Ming Cha, which markets its teas in stylish round silver tins and also offers beautiful gift packs with teas sealed inside cylindrical glass tubes. Choose from First Flush Longjin, Phoenix Supreme, Teguanyin Supreme, Yunnan Tippy Puerh, Wuy Yan Cha, green oolong, Mandarin Orchid, Golden Tip Puerh, and X'tra Old Tippy Puerh. Other departments of Selfridges store are well worth visiting for accessories, cosmetics, furnishings, stationery, shoes, and all the latest fashions.

Selfridges stocks teas from many vendors, including the Hong Kong company Ming Cha, which offers tea gift packs inside cylindrical glass tubes (photo below).

• Mon.-Wed. and Fri.-Sat. 9:30am-8pm, Thurs. 9:30am-9pm, Sun. 11:30am-8pm • Nearest tubes: Bond Street, Marble Arch • Buses: 10, 73, 113, 137, 139, 189 • Tel: 020 7318 3405 • Food retail area of department store with selection of teas • Major credit cards • www.selfridges.co.uk

Whittard of Chelsea T-Zone, Carnaby Street
Neighborhood: Chelsea
43 Carnaby Street, London W1F7EA

Whittard has shops throughout London selling an assortment of teas and coffees, but the two Whittard T-Zones (the other is in central London) deal only in tea. Here, shoppers may blend and flavor their own teas, beginning with three base teas (Ceylon black, China black and China green) and adding their own personal selection of flavorings and essential oils. It's smart, streamlined, and a hands-on experience that brings the art of tea drinking to life. The T-Zone shops also offer tea wares and books.

• Mon.-Sat. 10am-7:30pm, Sun. 11am-6:30pm
• Nearest tube: Oxford Circus • Buses: 3, 6, 15, 23 • Tel: 020 7439 0095 • Tea retail store with do-it-yourself blending area upstairs • Major credit cards • www.whittard.com

Whittard of Chelsea, Oxford Street
Neighborhood: Northwest London and West End
38 Oxford Street, London, W1D 1BA

One of the more than twenty Whittard shops in London selling tea and coffee.

• Mon.-Sat. 10am-8pm, Sun. 11am-7pm • Nearest tube: Tottenham Court Road, Oxford Circus •

Madame Tussaud's waxworks (photo right) is one of the most visited tourist attractions in London. It is on Marylebone Road and accessible from the Baker Street tube station.

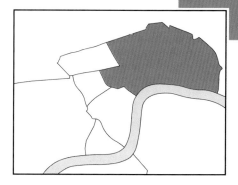

Soho to the City

*Soho, Covent Garden, Bloomsbury,
Strand, Holborn, The City*

If you want to absorb the essence of modern London, these are the areas to visit. Soho and Covent Garden buzz with life, Strand is home to several major theatres, Holborn reflects the importance of the British legal system, and the City (the name of a historic area at the heart of London) is still the center for banking and commerce. The area is filled with tea stores and market stalls, along with fascinating historical links back through 350 years of tea in London.

The Montague on the Gardens
Neighborhood: Bloomsbury
15 Montague Street, Bloomsbury, London,
WC1B 5BJ

The Montague on the Gardens is housed in a Grade II listed building made up of no less than nine Georgian houses dating back to 1815. In more recent times, members of a 20th century literary circle, the Bloomsbury Group – including such luminaries as Virginia Woolf, Clive Bell, Vanessa Bell, and Duncan Grant – stayed in one of the houses and held meetings here. The building has its tea connections, too. The houses were once part of the Duke of Bedford's estate, and it was the Seventh Duchess of Bedford, Anna Maria, who gave Afternoon Tea its name in early 1800s.

At tea time, there are many choices including traditional Afternoon Tea and Champagne Tea.

An ornate gate (photo, opposite) marks the entrance to London's thriving Chinatown enclave.

The Cream Tea features freshly baked scones, clotted cream, and jam, while the Cherry Cream Tea comes with cherry scones instead of plain. Strawberry Cream Tea has scones, jam and cream, and a bowl of English strawberries with a scoop of vanilla ice cream. For devoted chocolate eaters, there is the Chocolate Tea with finger sandwiches, freshly baked chocolate scones with Devonshire clotted cream, white and dark chocolate dipping sauce, and chocolate French pastries. To accompany any or all of these, choose Earl Grey, English Breakfast, Darjeeling, China Green, Russian Caravan, Yunnan, Assam, White Chocolate and Caramel Fudge tea, Vanilla Classic, or a fruit or herbal infusion.

• Afternoon tea served every day, 3-6pm • Nearest tubes: Tottenham Court Road, Russell Square • Buses: 8, 25, 242 to Museum Street, or 59, 68, 168, 188 to Southampton Row • Tel: 020 7637 1001 • Reservations recommended • Major credit cards • www.montaguehotel.com • Afternoon Tea, Cream Tea, Cherry Cream Tea, Strawberry Cream Tea, Chocolate Tea, Champagne Tea, tea by the pot • ££

Royal Opera House, Floral Hall
Neighborhood: Covent Garden
Bow Street, Covent Garden, London, WC2E 9DD

The Floral Hall at the Royal Opera House usually serves as the bar for opera-goers and occasionally is used for musical events. But about twenty times each year, the bar is dismantled and the entire space becomes a Friday evening dance floor for tea dance fans. Tickets, which include tea and biscuits, can be obtained for a small fee from the booking office. That admits you to join the avid dancers and tea drinkers who gather to try the tango, foxtrot, waltz, quickstep, and cha cha. Come in and jive to your heart's content. Live music is provided by the excellent nine-piece Royal Opera House Dance Band, and the entire event is sponsored by Tea Direct, a Fair Trade tea company. The space itself is glorious – high glass-domed ceiling, plenty of room, views out over the streets of Covent Garden, and, of course, the exciting link with all the performances of opera and ballet that take place in the building. Don your best frock or tux, polish up your shoes, and take to the floor.

• Tea dances held 1-3pm on Fridays when the Floral Hall is available; call for dates, details, and bookings • Nearest tubes: Covent Garden, Charing Cross, Leicester Square • Buses: 59, 168, 68, 1, 171 to Lancaster Place, then walk • Tel: 020 7212 9410 • Major credit cards • info. royaloperahouse.org • £

The tea dance, a beloved British pastime in the days before World War II, is making a comeback in the city.

The Savoy Hotel
Neighborhood: Strand
Strand, London, WC2R 0EU

The very name of the Savoy is famous, and within its walls, the Thames Foyer has its own reputation. In the large room where Noel Coward once played, where Caruso sang and Anna Pavlova danced in *Cabaret*, the resident pianist now plays while relaxed guests sit back and enjoy tea. In the past few years, the hotel staff has worked to develop a high quality afternoon tea worthy of the setting.

The Savoy's Afternoon Tea brings a selection of sandwiches with a variety of interesting fillings, tea cakes, and scones with jam and clotted cream, and a selection of pretty pastries. The Champagne Tea adds a glass of bubbly to those selections. The Theatre Tea is more hearty, a sort of high tea tailored to those with evening tickets for theatre, cinema, or concert. It offers English beef tea, Mulligatawny or London Particular en demi tasse, leek and Stilton quiche, miniature Cornish pasty, steak and ale pie with Yorkshire pudding crust, Welsh rarebit with English mustard, and potted Morecombe Bay shrimps with toast.

Those are followed by Red Leicester cheese scones with fig and apple relish and saffron yogurt, bread and butter pudding, apple and sultana crumble spiced with nutmeg, Savoy sherry trifle with crème Chantilly, cinnamon flavored carrot and orange cake, and After Eight chocolate crumpets with mint jelly. Of course, you don't have to be planning a theatrical evening to tuck into this savory and sweet treat.

Just come and make it your evening meal, then relax and sit for a while over a glass of wine or champagne.

The tea list is impressive, and several of the teas have imaginative names. You can choose from Tiger Hill Nilgiri, Lapsang Souchong, Earl Grey, Sencha Kyoto Cherry Rose, Crime of Passion, Orange Blossom Oolong, Ceylon Dimbula St. Coombs, and Ceylon Kenmare. Also: Rose Congou Emperor, Hummingbird Vanilla, Mango Mist, Savoy Special Blend (Indian, Ceylon, Kenya), Chun Mee, White Monkey Paw, Jasmine, Sencha Fukujyu, Darjeeling Margaret's Hope, Darjeeling Castleton, Assam Gingia, Assam Bukhial, Pai Mu Tan, 100 Monkeys, decaffeinated Irish Breakfast, decaffeinated Earl Grey, Yummy Berry and Tutti Frutti (for children), and several herbal and fruit infusions.

• Afternoon Tea served in the Thames Foyer, two sittings on weekdays: Mon.-Fri. 2-3:30pm and 4-5:30pm. Three sittings on weekends: Sat.-Sun. noon-1:30pm, 2-3:30pm, and 4-5:30pm. High Tea served every day, 5:30pm and 7:30pm • Nearest tubes: Charing Cross, Temple, Covent Garden • Buses: 139, 1, 59, 68, 168, 26, 171, 341, 172, 76 • Tel: 020 7836 4343 • Reservations essential; call 020 7420 2356 or e-mail: svy. dining@fairmont.com • Major credit cards • www.fairmont.com/savoy • Afternoon Tea, Champagne Tea, Theatre High Tea • £££

St. Martin's Lane Hotel
Neighborhood: Covent Garden
45 St Martin's Lane, London, WC2N 4HX

Tea time at St. Martin's Lane is worthwhile simply for the chance to take in the witty, quirky decor and unusual setting. Designed by Philippe Starck, each area of the hotel is an innovative, smile-provoking mixture of surreal, baroque, ultramodern, and cheeky. In the lobby, an outsized silver vase stands against one wall and a row of giant gold teeth serve as a spot to perch. A larger-than-life gilded chaise is draped luxuriously with a pashmina, and a chess set with pieces two feet tall is arranged to one side.

Ahead of you is the light bar with its spindly-legged tables and stools, and to the left of that is the Asia de Cuba Restaurant, where tea is served. The room is broken up by several large round pillars, each one decorated in its own style. One is stacked with books, radios, and other objects, and another is decked with lots of potted plants. There's a quilted pillar, and one covered with black and white photos. Lighting is provided from light bulbs dangling from long exposed wires over each beech table. The overall effect is pleasingly unusual.

The quirky decor at St. Martin's Lane Hotel is a smile-provoking mixture of baroque and cheeky. A row of giant gold teeth serve as a spot to perch, and a chess set with pieces two feet tall is arranged to one side.

"A jewel-box counter is perfectly designed to display the selection of fine pastries and little cakes – raspberry brûlée, chocolate mille-feuilles, wild strawberry and lychee Diplomat with milk chocolate, and violet and white chocolate gelée."

The Waldorf Hilton Hotel, Homage Patisserie

Neighborhood: Strand
22, The Aldwych, London WC2B 4DD

The Waldorf Hotel opened in Edwardian London at a time when the ultra-rich pursued an often frivolous and indulgent lifestyle, taking tea to the genteel sound of string quartets and tea dance orchestras in expansive hotel lounges and Palm Courts. The beautiful Palm Court at the Waldorf Hilton no longer hosts such events, and tea now is served in the Homage Patisserie, a smaller area at the front of the hotel that is intimate and hushed. It's a quietly personal room where you feel you could perhaps discuss your deepest secrets with a trusted companion.

The entrance to the Patisserie is from the hotel lobby with its gleaming, pressed metal finish, and the tea room draws you in with its soft lights, gauze drapes at the windows, rich fabrics, and inviting period furniture. A jewel-box counter is perfectly designed to display the selection of fine pastries and little cakes – raspberry brûlée, chocolate mille-feuilles, wild strawberry and lychee Diplomat with milk chocolate, and violet and white chocolate gelée. The menu leaves you free to choose any of those or any of the sandwiches. You might decide on pink shrimp with dill mayonnaise, honey-roasted ham with mustard, roast beef with horseradish butter, or smoked salmon and cream cheese. You could order the full Afternoon Tea with a selection of sandwiches, scones and pastries, or the Cream Tea with scones and a tea of your choice.

The tea list includes Royal English, Assam, Darjeeling, Orange Blossom Oolong, Jasmine, Earl Grey, Dimbula Ceylon, Lapsang Souchong, Genmaicha, and a few infusions. Each is brewed in a white porcelain pot and poured through a small tea strainer in the old-fashioned way.

• Tea served every day 9am-9pm. Afternoon Tea served every day 2:30-5:30pm • Nearest tubes: Charing Cross, Holborn, Temple • Buses: 139, 1, 59, 68, 168, 26, 171, 341, 172, 76 • Tel: 020 7759 4080 • Reservations recommended • Major credit cards • www.homagegrandsalon.co.uk • Afternoon Tea, Cream Tea, Tea à la carte, tea by the pot • ££

75

All the teas are bagged, organic, and arrive at the table in sleek white porcelain pots. The food menu is an appetizing mixture of sandwiches such as salmon and cream cheese with mache lettuce; avocado, rocket and parmesan; and the rather more substantial club sandwich or steak ciabatta with tomato, caramelized onions, fried egg and BBQ sauce. If you fancy something sweet to accompany your tea, there are homemade cookies, white chocolate and blueberry cheesecake, scones with homemade jam and cream, Cuban coffee brownies with chocolate fudge sauce, and mini Mexican doughnuts filled with butterscotch sauce. Not the traditional tea menu but deliciously satisfying.

• Afternoon tea served in the Asia de Cuba restaurant every day, 3-5pm • Nearest tubes: Charing Cross, Leicester Square • Tel: 020 7300 5500 • Reservations recommended • Major credit cards • www.stmartinslane.com • Tea à la carte, tea by the pot • ££

Shopping Sites for Tea Lovers

Algerian Coffee Store
Neighborhood: Soho
52 Old Compton Street, London, W1D 4PB

The window of this little shop is packed full of teas, coffees, and brewing equipment, offering a taste of what awaits inside. It is a boutique-sized Aladdin's cave where shoppers can find just about any type of loose tea and infusion, plus teabags, mugs, teapots, caddies, and filters. Well trained staff members are friendly and helpful and will guide you through your purchases of single estate teas and blends from India (at least five from Assam, fourteen from Darjeeling, one from Nilgiri), Sri Lanka (six from the different areas), China (whites, greens, blacks, congous, display teas, jasmines, and other flavored teas), Taiwan (at least fourteen), and Japan (five or more including Sencha, Bancha, Kokeicha, Japanese Cherry). You will also find flavored syrups, drinking chocolate, quality chocolate bars, chocolate covered figs, and chocolate coated coffee beans, all of which are available by mail order.

• Mon.-Wed. 9am-7pm, Thur.-Fri. 9am-9pm, Sat. 9am-8pm • Nearest tubes: Leicester Square, Piccadilly Circus • Tel: 020 7437 2480 • Major credit cards • www.algcoffee.co.uk • Retail store selling loose teas and teabags

The Drury Tea and Coffee Company, though now located on New Row, originally took its name from Drury Lane, immortalized in a nursery tune as home of the muffin man.

Drury Tea and Coffee Company Ltd.
Neighborhood: Covent Garden
3 New Row (off St. Martin's Lane), London, WC2N 4LH

In 1936, three Italian brothers by the name of Olmi set up a tea company in Covent Garden's Drury Lane, and ten years later the business changed its name to the Drury Tea and Coffee Company. The shop is ideally placed for anyone meandering through the streets around Trafalgar Square and Covent Garden, and it is worth a visit as the tea list totals more than one hundred different varieties. Included are white, green, oolong, and black teas from China, oolongs and greens from Taiwan, green teas from Japan, black teas from Sri Lanka, India and Africa, decaffeinated teas, and several traditional blends such as Russian Caravan and Imperial Earl Grey. The shop also stocks teapots of different sizes, biscuits, jams, and chocolates.

• Mon.-Sat. 9am-6pm • Nearest tube: Charing Cross, Leicester Square, Covent Garden • Tel: 0207836 1960 • www.drury.uk.com • Major credit cards • Tea retail store selling wide range of loose and bagged teas

The Silver Vaults
Neighborhood: Holborn
Chancery House, Chancery Lane, London WC2A 1QS

There are thirty-seven individual dealers in this warren of fascinating shops, and it is both fun and instructive to browse through the shops, discovering beautiful table wares and decorative objects. You will find Chinese tea kettles made in Oriental style but for use on British tea tables, European tea kettles, and silver tea sets with tray, teapot, hot water jug, sugar bowl, and milk jug.

There are plenty of specialty items including sweetmeat dishes, caddies, caddy spoons, teaspoons, mote spoons, pastry forks and tea knives, cakes stands, muffin dishes, and

> "Yauatcha is only the second Chinese restaurant in Europe to achieve Michelin recogniton for excellence...and the entire experience here is of modern Oriental tea drinking with a sophisticated European twist."

Yauatcha

Neighborhood: Soho
15-17 Broadwick Street, Soho, London, W1F 0DL

Yauatcha (prounced *yow-AT-cha*) is only the second Chinese restaurant in Europe to achieve Michelin recognition for excellence, and the other acclaimed eatery - Hakkasan - shares the same owner, Alan Yau. He also is the owner of Busaba Eathai (Thai treats) and set up the very popular Wagamama restaurants (Japanese cuisine) which he recently sold.

Yauatcha includes a Chinese dim sum and noodle restaurant in the basement, with a Chinese tea house on the ground floor. The selection of two dozen or so different varieties of dim sum have been devised by a master of Chinese food, Wong Chiu Chun. Preparation of the tea list was given an equal amount of care under the supervision of specialist Hsieh Chih Chang from Taipei. The current tea consultant, Master King, also from Taipei, is responsible for training staff members and developing the impressive list or teas. From Taiwan, you'll find Four Seasons Oolong, Taipei Green, and Jasmine. From China's Fujian province, try Huang Jin Gui or Wuyi Yan Cha - Shui Xian (roast). From Yunnan, Tian Hong black tea and Dark Puerh. (If you need advice, ask Sonia – she's an excellent waitress and loves to chat through your choices with you.) All the teas are expertly brewed in the pantry, and leaves are removed before the pot is delivered to the table.

The entire experience here is of modern Oriental tea drinking with a sophisticated European twist. The decor is modern stylish Asian but with European influences – lots of blue glass, streamlined simple tables, minimalist flower arrangements in sleek porcelain vases, and a startlingly beautiful white marble counter where the eye-catching patisserie is laid out to tempt. Enjoy any of the treats offered in the tea house or take some home. Make sure you try the brightly-colored, yoyo-shaped, melt-in-the-mouth macaroons.

• Tea house open every day 10am-11pm; restaurant open Mon.-Wed. noon-2:30pm and 6pm-midnight, Thurs.-Sun. 11:30am-midnight • Nearest tubes: Leicester Square, Piccadilly Circus, Oxford Circus • Buses: 7, 8, 10, 55, 73, 98 to Oxford Street/Wardour Street, then walk • Tel: 020 7494 8888 • Reservations essential • Major credit cards • ££

muffineers (shakers rather like sugar casters but designed for sprinkling cinnamon sugar on hot buttered muffins).

This is the biggest collection of silver in the world, so if you are looking for antique tea wares, it's the ideal spot. The dealers will take time to discuss exactly what you are looking for, and they will be remarkably knowledgeable about pieces that catch your eye. Don't miss Vault 24, owned by Stephen and Jeremy Stodel. They specialize in Chinese and European tea wares (Tel: 020 7405 7009).

• Mon.-Fri. 9am-5:30pm, Sat. 9am-1pm • Nearest tube: Chancery lane • Buses: 68, 168, 171 • Tel: 020 7242 3844 • Major credit cards • Dealers selling silver table wares • www.thesilvervaults.com

The Tea House
Neighborhood: Covent Garden
15 Neal Street, Covent Garden, London, WC2H 9PU

Set in one of Covent Garden's busiest streets, where tourists mingle with locals to roam through eclectic shops, the Tea House has been doing a roaring trade in loose and bagged teas since 1983. Christina Smith originally opened the business because she saw tea being marketed simply as a souvenir product, and she wanted people to really like tea rather than buying it as a tourist curiosity.

Despite the small space, the shop is packed with all sorts of teas, brewing equipment, tins, books, and cozies. On the left as you enter, look for strainers, filters, infusers, caddy spoons, timers, drip catchers, and other tea bits and bobs. In the far corner on the ground floor, more than 100 different loose teas and infusions are stacked on shelves that run floor to ceiling.

Glass jars behind the counter hold precious specialty teas such as Jasmine Dragon Phoenix Pearl. Along the front of the shop and up the stairs are jars of jam, tins of biscuits, mugs, teapots, gift packs, and tea tins. As you reach the top of the stairs, you will find a wide selection of colorful teapots in different sizes, mugs, cups and saucers, books, cozies, Yixing teapots, and more. This little shop is a tea treasure trove.

• Mon.-Sat. 10am-7pm, Sun. 11am-6pm • Nearest tubes: Covent Garden, Leicester Square • Tel: 020 7240 7539 • Retail shop selling teas, tea accessories, teapots, and tea books • Major credit cards

Twinings
Neighborhood: Strand
216 Strand, London, WC2R 1AP

In 1706, Thomas Twining purchased Tom's Coffee House in Devereux Court, just off Strand, and set up as a coffee and tea merchant. The area was perfect for his new business as many wealthy families had relocated here after the Great Fire of London. His list of customers soon included such eminent names as Earl Cardigan, Lord Lichfield, the painter William Hogarth, and members of the royal family.

By 1717, Thomas had purchased three small buildings next door to the original shop. One of these became 216 Strand, the company's famous London address, directly opposite the imposing gothic building that houses London Law Courts and at the point where Strand becomes Fleet Street. Almost three hundred years and ten generations later, the Twinings family is still selling tea from this historic location and, of course, in stores and supermarkets all over the world.

A golden lion and two men sit above the front door, guarding the entrance to the original shop. Inside, portraits from many generations of the family line the upper sections of the shop wall and gaze down on today's customers. The shop still sells a wide range of loose and bagged teas and infusions and offers a range of other tea merchandise – teapots, cups, mugs, books, biscuits, cakes, and chocolates. At the back of the shop there is a small museum that documents the history of the family, along with some fabulous examples of tea caddies and more unusual items from the world of tea.

Step inside the historic walls of Twinings for shopping and a chance to experience 300 years of tea history in England.

After you're finished at Twinings, take a short walk up Fleet Street to the east and visit Samuel Johnson's house in Gough Square. You'll be steeped in British history.

• Mon.-Fri. 9:30am-4:30pm • Nearest tube: Temple • Bus: 4, 15, 26, 68, 76, 168, 171, 172, 176 • Tel: 020 7353 3511 or 0870 241 3667 • Retail shop selling loose and bagged teas and tea related items • www.twinings.com • Major credit cards

Whittard of Chelsea T-Zone, Covent Garden
Neighborhood: Covent Garden
38 Covent Garden Market, London, WC2E 8RF

Whittard has shops throughout London selling an assortment of teas and coffees, but the two Whittard T-Zones (the other is in Carnaby Street) deal only in tea. The shop is designed to offer tea lovers a wide range of specialty teas and to give shoppers the chance to blend and flavor their own teas.

A specially-designed blending counter holds three large bowls with the base teas – Ceylon black, China black and China green – and around the edges are smart metal bowls filled with a selection of flavorings usually blended with tea. You can pick and choose from rosehips, hibiscus, orange peel, cinnamon, mint, elderberries, lemongrass, apple pieces, papaya, sunflowers, jasmine blossoms, rose petals, and mallow flowers. Scoop them into your chosen leaf to create your own individual blend. Also provided are bottles of essential oils such as bergamot, mango, lemon, strawberry, vanilla, peach, and lemon, which can be sprayed onto the leaf and blended inside the cocktail-style shakers provided. It's all very smart and streamlined. For children and adventurous tea drinkers, it provides a hands-on experience that brings the art of tea drinking to life.

On shelves near the blending area, there are rare teas in glass jars so that the leaf is clearly visible to those browsing. Around the room are all sorts of other tea things – Chinese earthenware teapots and drinking bowls, glass pots with their own infuser baskets, tea bricks, compressed teas in their round Chinese boxes, and books about tea, including one called *Infusion* by Whittard tea taster and buyer Giles Hilton, the tea lover and expert who dreamt up the idea of T-Zone.

• Mon.-Sat. 10am-7:30pm, Sun. 11am-6:30pm
• Nearest tubes: Covent Garden, Holborn, Leicester Square • Buses: 59 to Lancaster Place, then walk • Tel: 020 7379 6599 • Tea retail store with do-it-yourself blending area upstairs • Major credit cards • www.whittard.com

Whittard of Chelsea, Regent Street
Neighborhood: Regent Street, Central London
65/67 Regent Street, London, W1B 4DZ

Space is at a premium in this busy shopping street running from Piccadilly Circus to Oxford Circus, and Whittard is crammed into a little triangular site constantly packed with busy tourists eager to stock up with tea gifts to carry back home. The range of products includes more London and British souvenirs than any other Whittard's branch: little buses filled with tea, round tins of teabags decorated with the Underground logo, and tins of Scottish shortbread.

There is virtually no coffee, but the very limited shelf space does manage to offer teapots, infusers, mugs, and gift packs, as well as a range of loose and bagged teas. Staff members always have a flask of the tea of the day, offering tasters to anyone who wants to try a different tea.

• Mon.-Sat. 9:30am-8pm, Sun. 10am-8pm • Nearest tube: Piccadilly Circus • Buses: 3, 12, 88, 139, 453, A1 • Tel: 020 7437 4175

Whittard of Chelsea, Coventry Street
Neighborhood: Piccadilly Circus, Central London & City
Unit 7, 13 Coventry Street, London, W1V 7SE

• Mon.-Fri. 10am-10pm, Sat.-Sun. 10am-11pm • Nearest tube: Piccadilly Circus • Buses: 19, 38, A1 • Tel: 020 7734 8217

Yum cha is a Chinese phrase that means to have tea. Because Chinese hospitality dictates that a drink should not be served without something to eat, the phrase has come to mean chatting with friends over a cup of tea and dim sum (tea snacks).

Whittard of Chelsea, Strand
Neighborhood: Strand, Central London & City
435 Strand, London, WC2R 0QN

• Mon.-Sat. 9am-7pm, Sun. 11am-6pm • Nearest tube: Charing Cross • Buses: 6, 9, 13, 15, 139 • Tel: 020 7379 6378

Whittard of Chelsea, Moorgate
Neighborhood: Central London & City
74 Moorgate, London, EC2M 6SE

• Mon.-Fri. 8am-7pm, closed Sat.-Sun. • Nearest tube: Moorgate • Buses: 21, 43, 76, 133, 141, 214 • Tel: 020 7638 4248

Yumchaa, Leadenhall Market
Neighborhood: The City
Leadenhall Street, London

Yumchaa is a dynamic tea venture run by high-energy youthful entrepreneurs. The Yumchaa teas are unusual flavored blends of black, green, rooibos, and white teas with clever names such as Chelsea Chai, Enchanted Forest, and Ginseng Guardian. Yumchaa has three other locations in Camden Market, St. James's Market, and Porto-bello Road. Check flagship listing in Camden.

• Wed.-Fri. 11:30am-3:30pm • Nearest tubes: Bank, Monument • Buses: 35, 47, 48, 133, 149 • Market stall selling flavored loose leaf teas and infusions • Check with banker's card, cash • www.yumchaa.co.uk

An 1860 engraving from Harper's Weekly *(photo below) depicts Dr. Samuel Johnson surrounded by admirers at a tea party hosted by his good friend, Mrs. Thrale (in the green dress). Johnson's house now is revered for its significance in the history of literature and also embodies the British devotion to tea.*

On the Tea Trail in London

Samuel Johnson's House
Neighborhood: Strand
17 Gough Square, London, EC4 3DE

Samuel Johnson earned literary fame with the 1755 publication of his *Dictionary of the English Language*. He was a man who loved words, and he also had a passion for tea. His home, a fascinating piece of English history, is a short distance from the Twining's shop and well worth the walk up to Fleet Street. It is tucked away in a side alley, so be sure to watch for the historical marker or ask directions.

Dr. Johnson described himself as a "hardened and shameless tea-drinker, who has for many years diluted his meals with only the infusion of this fascinating plant." He lived in Gough Square from 1748 to 1759 and compiled the greater part of his famous *Dictionary* in a room on the top floor of the house. His choice of this house was influenced by a need to be close to the printer who would produce the *Dictionary*, a man named William Strahan whose business was on New Street Square.

Johnson received many visitors at the house, and his friend, Arthur Murray, wrote, "His house was filled with a succession of visitors till four or five in the evening. During the whole time he presided at his tea-table." On display in a glass cabinet upstairs is a tea set that belonged to Johnson's friend, Mrs. Thrale.

The house was badly damaged during the Second World War, first by fire in 1940 when the roof and the Dictionary Attic were completely burnt out, again by fire in 1941, and in 1944 when a flying bomb hit. Despite those disasters, the house continued to stand, and today it embodies a strong link with the past. During the war, the firemen who stood ready to fight fires caused by bombing were not allowed into the service clubs used by the other forces. The curator of Dr. Johnson's house was granted permission by Lord Harmsworth, chairman of the body responsible for the house, to allow the building's use in offering relaxation and rest for the firemen and women. According to one fireman based there, the curator was "seldom seen without teapot in hand providing practical comfort to her local firemen." The house has since been restored, and visitors can readily envision many aspects of life in Johnson's time.

• From April-Sept., hours are 11am-5:30pm Mon.-Sat. From Oct.-Mar., hours are 11am-5pm Mon.-Sat. • Nearest tube: Blackfriars, Chancery Lane, Temple • Buses: 4, 11, 15, 23, 26, 45, 63, 76, 172 • Tel: 020 7353 3745 • Small admission charge • Reservations necessary for groups of more than 10 • www.drjh.dircon.co.uk

83

Southbank
to Greenwich

Waterloo, Borough, Greenwich

Since the opening of the Channel Tunnel and its rail link to continental Europe, the area around Waterloo Station has become a vibrant blend of tourist venues, popular restaurants, and chic residences created out of former office blocks and civic buildings. Farther from the heart of the city, Greenwich is an elegant haven, complete with riverside walks and a sweeping park. The fine Georgian architecture of the National Maritime Museum, Royal Naval College, Queen's House, and Royal Observatory lend a calm serenity to the landscape.

Bramah Museum of Tea and Coffee
Neighborhood: Southwark
40 Southwark St., London SE1 1UN

The Bramah Museum celebrates the commercial and social history of tea and coffee for the 400 years since those beverages arrived in Europe from the Far East and Africa. The museum tea room serves cream tea (scones with clotted cream and jam, cake, and the tea of choice) and afternoon tea (cucumber sandwiches, hot crumpets, cake, and the tea of choice).

The upper walkways of the Tower Bridge offer remarkable views of the city, and the neo-Gothic towers house a remarkable array of exhibits, presentations, and artifacts devoted to the history of the bridge.

• Museum open daily 10am-6pm • Bus: 381 Waterloo Station, RV1 • Nearest tube: London Bridge (take platform-level exit to Borough St.) • Tel: 020 7403 5650 • E-mail: bramah@btconnection.com • Major credit cards • www.bramahmuseum.co.uk • Reservations recommended • £

Marriott County Hall
Neighborhood: Waterloo
Westminster Bridge Road, London, SE1 7PB

The vast building that today houses the Marriott Hotel was once County Hall, providing office space for all the decision makers and politicians who governed London and its environs. Many an adult in London has youthful memories of of singing in choirs here or appearing before boards who chose students to be awarded special trips abroad. The corridors then probably seemed rather daunting. Today, all is plush, luxurious, and quiet, designed to make your visit as peaceful and enjoyable as possible.

Even so, traces of the past remain. The Library, where afternoon tea is served, was originally the library for the members of the Greater London Council and, with bookcases and alcoves still in place, the opulence and grandeur of the room have been well preserved. From the window, you can see the Thames and beyond to Westminster, Big Ben, and tourist activity on Westminster Bridge. On days when the Library is booked for a private function, tea is served in the Rotunda Lounge, which also offers excellent views over the river.

Afternoon tea consists of assorted finger sandwiches, freshly baked scones served with strawberry preserves and clotted cream, and a selection of pastries. The tea list offers Darjeeling, Earl Grey, Assam, Lapsang Souchong, Jasmine, Yunnan, Traditional English, and a few herbal and fruit infusions. A glass of Dappier Champagne will turn your tea into a special occasion.

• Afternoon Tea served every day, 2:30-5:30pm in the Library or Rotunda Lounge • Nearest tube: Westminster, Waterloo • Buses: 4, 12, 26, 76, 148, 172 to Waterloo Bridge and walk, or RV1 to the London Eye • Tel: 020 7902 8047 • Major credit cards • www.marriott.com • Afternoon tea, tea à la carte, tea by the pot • ££

Shopping Sites for Tea Lovers

Ceylon One
Neighborhood: Southeast London
Borough Market, London, SE1

Rob Green sells only organic single estate teas from plantations in Sri Lanka's Uva district and maintains very close personal links with the estates from which he buys. At one time, he lived with a Sri Lankan family and still visits them when he can. Ten percent of all profits from Ceylon One are given back to local Sri Lankan charities to help support health and education projects that aid street children and workers on the plantations.

Rob's range of teas includes English Breakfast, Ceylon, Orange Pekoe, Jasmine, Earl Grey, Lady Grey, Royal Chai, Green Tea Lemon, and Green Tea Orange. Borough Market is in itself a colorful and historic part of London. On a Saturday morning, it is alive with shoppers, sightseers, families with their children, and busy stall holders selling an amazing range of fruit, vegetables, bread, cakes, wine, meat, fish, flowers, olives, and, of course, tea. To find Rob, approach the market from Stoney Street, turn right into the market and follow one of the passages that lead under the railway arches, across Canterbury Street, and through to the courtyard. Rob's stall is on the left side of the courtyard.

From Waterloo Station, an interesting riverside walk to the east takes you past Gabriel's Wharf, the Oxo Tower, Tate Modern, Shakespeare's Globe, and Southwark Cathedral. You'll find the huge Borough Market where tea merchants join the fruit, vegetable, and grocery retailers every Friday and Saturday.

• Fri. noon-6pm, Sat: 9am-4pm • Nearest tubes: Borough, London Bridge • Tel: Market = 020 7407 1002/Ceylon One = 079 1706 1711 • Cash only, credit cards for online store • www.ceylon1.com • Market stall selling Ceylon organic loose teas

East Teas
Neighborhood: Southeast London
Borough Market, London, SE1

The two people behind East Teas are Tim d'Offay and Alex Fraser. Both fell in love with tea a long time ago – Alex Fraser in a Manchester restaurant in the 1950s when he tasted some Chinese tea, and Tim while traveling around Japan and Taiwan when he was a student. Both have a real passion for the teas they sell. They can tell you about the plantations that provide their teas, the people who work there, and the character of the different leaves.

East Teas' stall at Borough market attracts a steady stream of eager and inquisitive customers every week and is usually manned by Alex who happily hands out tasters, information, and enlightenment in equal portions. The list includes rare and wonderful teas such as Snow Jewel (a silver needle type tea from China), Jade Oolong, Amber Oolong and White Tip Oolong from Taiwan, Organic Sencha and Guricha from Japan, and Nokcha, a green Korean tea that has the most divine flavor with hints of caramel and sweet biscuits. Borough Market is a treat in itself, but to find such dedicated tea retailers in the midst of the buzzing throng of stall holders and shoppers is a real thrill. Don't miss having a chat with Alex.

• Fri. noon-6pm, Sat. 9am-4pm • Nearest tubes: Borough, London Bridge • Tel: 020 7394 0226 • www.eastteas.com • Cash and checks with banker's card • Market stall selling teas from China, Taiwan, Japan and Korea

On the Tea Trail in London

Butlers Wharf
Neighborhood: Southeast London
Butlers Wharf, London SE1

Built in 1873, Butlers Wharf sits on the southern waterfront of the Thames just east of Tower Bridge. The fascinating area, with its restaurants, art galleries, wine bars, and shops, was once London's largest tea warehousing complex. Refurbishment began in the 1980s, and many of the original features have been incorporated into the modern businesses that thrive here.

Look above as you walk along in Shad Thames, and you will see the iron walkways that linked the various warehouses. It's not hard to imagine porters trundling heavy tea chests on trolleys across those high bridges. The name of the Shad Thames area is said to be a corruption of St. John at Thames, a reference to the Knights Templar who once controlled the area. There are plenty of other places to visit in this area – the Design Museum, Tower Bridge Museum, HMS Belfast, the Tower of London, and St. Katherine's Dock on the north side of the river.

Butlers Wharf was built in 1873 as London's largest tea warehousing complex. The area now hosts restaurants, art galleries, wine bars, and shops.

• Nearest tubes: Tower, London Bridge • Buses: RV1, 47, 188

Cutty Sark Clipper Ship

Neighborhood: Greenwich
King William Walk,
Greenwich, London, SE10
9HT

The rail ride from central London out to Greenwich is not a long one, but in many ways, the trip will give you passage across more than one hundred years of time. For sitting there in dry dock beside the river is the magnificent Cutty Sark clipper ship, a testament to one of the most glamorous and memorable eras in the history of tea. Breathtakingly beautiful, the Cutty Sark is the world's last surviving example of an extreme clipper ship. It was on board this and other clippers that chests of tea arrived at the London docks in the 19th century.

Built in 1869, the Cutty Sark became famous for bringing the first tea crop to London each year from China with record speed. She plied the ocean from 1870 until 1877 and now rests at Greenwich, once the center of maritime

Britain. The Cutty Sark serves as a museum of maritime history and the tea trade. Visitors can admire her twenty-two miles of rigging and see cabins and galleys recreated to show how life was for sailors during long days at sea. Below deck is a collection of figureheads.

Beginning in the autumn of 2006, the Cutty Sark will undergo a three-year restoration and protection project. Plans call for portions of the ship to remain open to the public at all times. Special displays will be paired with hard-hat tours of the restoration work, showing a blend of traditional ship-building skills and modern technology.

After the official re-opening in 2009, the Cutty Sark will be displayed in a new setting with the dry dock covered in a spectacular glass sea. Visitors will have the opportunity to walk underneath the hull and experience the style of construction that was groundbreaking for the era. There will also be added emphasis on her days as a tea clipper. Visitors will have the opportunity to experience tea tasting in her cargo hold.

Visitors to the Cutty Sark museum can admire her twenty-two miles of rigging and see cabins and galleys recreated to show how life was for sailors during long days at sea.

• 10am-5pm every day except Christmas Eve, Christmas Day, and Boxing Day (Dec. 26); last admission 30 minutes before closing • Nearest tube: Cutty Sark (Docklands Light Railway) • Nearest railway station: Greenwich • Buses: 177, 180, 188, 199 • www.cuttysark.org.uk • Tel: 020 8858 3445 • Clipper ship museum, information about tea trade, gift shop selling tea

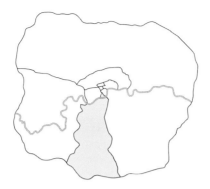

Western Reaches
of the Thames

Fulham, Putney, Wimbledon, Battersea

Many parts of London's southwestern
suburbs enjoy river views, open parks, and
common land where residents walk dogs,
fly kites, play team games, and relish the
space and fresh air. Nearby shopping malls
and high streets offer a good mix of
department stores, fashion outlets,
specialty food stores, and restaurants.

Aquasia at the Conrad
Neighborhood: West London
Chelsea Harbour, London, SW10 0XG

Situated beside the Thames at the river's western
reaches, this five-star hotel enjoys stunning views
of Chelsea Harbour and the dramatic skyline of
central London. The afternoon tea menu includes
traditional sandwiches, scones, and pastries presented in a modern style. Neat white side plates
are set on square blue platters that enhance the
marine theme of the decor. Pale wooden floors,
shiny silver pillars, and light that floods through
floor-to-ceiling windows add to the feeling that

*The neat white
side plates set
on square blue
platters give
guests at Aquasia
a sense of taking
tea on a very
plush yacht.*

guests are taking tea on a very plush yacht or motor launch.

The teas and infusions include a selection of herbal blends designed by an Ayurvedic yogi practitioner to detox, calm, or stimulate. Also listed are a flowery elegant Darjeeling from Jungpana, a single estate Assam from Mokalbarie, a Japanese sencha blended with flowers and fruits, Ceylon from the Uva district of Sri Lanka, and a rhubarb and vanilla infusion.

• Afternoon tea served in the restaurant every day, 3:30-6pm • Major credit cards • Nearest tube: Earls Court • Buses: C3, 239 • Tel: 020 7300 8443 • www.london.conradmeetings.com • Reservations possible but not essential • Afternoon Tea, tea à la carte • ££

O'Connors Tea Room
Neighborhood: Fulham
3-4 Broxholme House, New King's Road,
London, SW6 4AA

Hailing as he does from Dublin, Mark O'Connor has created a tea room that is Irish through and through. From the rich green front and awnings, to the Irish sausages, smoked salmon, and soda bread, everything smacks of the Emerald Isle. This feels like a room in an Irish family home. It is an unfussy, welcoming, down-to-earth, lived-in sort of place where the furniture is a mixture of domestic dining tables and chairs with a few Irish antiques scattered around. Everything has been planned to please the people who come here, but

there is no pretension of grandeur. It's good value, slightly quirky, and a treat for everyone, even if you're not Irish.

You can tuck into a hearty Irish breakfast of black pudding, bacon, poached eggs, Clonakilly sausages, mushrooms, tomato and soda bread, or enjoy the lighter fare of smoked salmon with scrambled eggs and chives plus soda bread. Enjoy a family-style lunch of shepherds pie or the Irish Ploughman's platter with cheddar cheese and Janet's homemade chutney. Afternoon tea brings sandwiches, scones, jam and clotted cream – and you can add a dish of Irish strawberries from Wexford if you have room.

To accompany all these satisfying foods, enjoy a good pot of Irish tea. Other beverages are available, but if you want alcohol, be sure to take your own. Don't miss the selection of Irish things for sale around the room and in the counter area. You'll see beautifully framed photos of Old Dublin, Irish greeting cards, Waterford crystal, Irish chocolates, relishes, chutneys, biscuits, and jams. This shop is full of character and delightful in daring to be different.

• Tea and food served every day beginning at 10am • Nearest tube: Fulham Broadway • Bus: 28 • Tel: 020 7736 2626 • Reservations possible • Major credit cards • £

Shopping Sites for Tea Lovers

Emma Bridgewater
Neighborhood: Fulham
739 Fulham Road, London SW6 5UL

Both the shapes and patterns of Emma Bridge-water's designs are very distinctive, and many British homes have a teapot or a few mugs, porridge bowls, cups, and saucers from this very popular pottery. The designs (all on a pale cream or white background) are bold, graphic, and fun. You can buy teapots covered with pink hearts, green clover leaves, multi-colored polka dots, bright red tulips, roses, or bold black lettering saying chirpy things such as 'Rise and Shine' or 'I love you more than chocolate.' The teapots are large, generous, sturdy, and chummy – perfect for a leisurely breakfast or a family tea around the kitchen table. Second location in Marylebone.

• Nearest tube; Fulham Broadway • Tel: 020 7371 5264 • www.emmabridgewater.co.uk • Major credit cards • Retail store selling pottery tea wares

Whittard of Chelsea, Battersea
Neighborhood: Battersea, South West London
73 Northcote Rd., Battersea, London, SW11 6PJ

One of the more than twenty Whittard shops scattered throughout London.

• Mon.-Sat. 9:30am-6pm, Sun. 11:30am-5pm • Buses: 35, 37 • Tel: 020 7924 2307

Whittard of Chelsea, Putney
Neighborhood: Putney, South West London
Unit 24, The Putney Exchange, High Street
Putney, London, SW15 1TW

• Mon.-Sat. 9am-6pm, Sun. 11am-5pm • Nearest tube: East Putney • Nearest station: Putney • Buses: 14, 39, 85, 93, 424 • Tel: 020 8789 9268

Whittard of Chelsea, Wimbledon
Neighborhood: Wimbledon, South West London
Unit 307, Centre Court, 4 Queens Road,
Wimbledon, London, SW19 8AY

• Mon.-Fri. 9am-7:30pm, Sat. 9am-7pm, Sun. 11am-5pm • Nearest tube: Wimbledon • Nearest station: Wimbledon • Tel: 020 8944 6943

Battersea was mentioned in Anglo-Saxon times as Badric's Isle or sometimes Patricsey, a Saxon phrase for Peter's river or water.

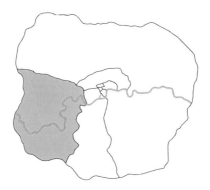

The Western Hamlets

Ealing, Chiswick, Kingston, Richmond, Kew

Throughout the open countryside to the west of London, a number of large mansions and palaces tell of an era when kings and queens and wealthy aristocrats preferred to reside at a comfortable distance from London's overcrowded center. Ham House, Richmond Park, Kew Gardens, and Hampton Court are the most famous. Each offers beautiful parkland and gardens in which to wander before tea.

Ham House

Neighborhood: Richmond
Ham, Richmond-upon-Thames, Surrey,
TW10 7RS

This Stuart house, built in 1610, was once home to the Duchess of Lauderdale, lady of fashion and close friend of Queen Catherine, who introduced tea drinking to the English aristocracy. The Duchess was amongst the first in England to acquire fine tea wares, and it's likely she used them to serve tea to the Queen in one of her two private closets (roughly equivalent to a small parlor). Visitors to the house can walk through these closets and see the Duchess' japanned chairs, Javanese tea table, porcelain tea bowls, and an exquisite Chinese porcelain teapot that dates to the third quarter of the 17th century. According to local legend, the spirit of the Duchess continues to haunt the house.

A ten-story Chinese pagoda (photo opposite) is one of the wonders awaiting visitors to the 300-acre Kew Gardens, among the most noted botanical gardens in the world.

95

• From Mar. 19-Oct. 30, house is open Mon.-Wed. and Sat.-Sun. 1-5pm. Garden open all year, Mon.-Wed. and Sat.-Sun. 11am-6pm • Nearest tube: Richmond • Nearest train station: Richmond • Buses: 371, K5 • Tel: 020 8940 1950 • Major credit cards • House with close links to 17th century tea drinking; tea may be taken in the garden tea room • £

Shopping Sites for Tea Lovers

Whittard of Chelsea, Ealing
Neighborhood: Ealing, West London
Unit 24, 67 Ealing Broadway Centre, Ealing, London, W5 5JY

One of the more than twenty Whittard shops serving tea and coffee throughout London.

• Mon.-Wed, and Fri.-Sat. 9:30am-6pm, Thurs. 9:30am-7pm, Sun. 11am-5pm • Nearest tube; Ealing Broadway • Buses: 207, 427 • Tel: 020 8840 8153

Whittard of Chelsea, Chiswick
Neighborhood: Chiswick, West London
322 Chiswick High Road, London, W4 5TA

Chiswick High Road is a busy shopping street for local residents, and this Whittard shop is set amongst high street banks, supermarkets, greengrocers, butchers, and shoe shops. Surprisingly, this is one of the larger Whittards, with far more floor space than the shops in the center of town. The shelves carry a wide range of coffee brewing machines, kettles, large coffee cups and saucers, plus spoons, scoops, and more teas than most other shops in the chain. There is a choice of unusual specialty teas from single estates, loose herbals (such as raspberry leaves and nettle), varied tea bags, a good range of biscuits and chocolates, teapots, and gift tea boxes.

• Mon.-Sat. 9:30am–6pm, Sun. 11:30am-5pm • Nearest tube: Chiswick Park • Buses: E3, 237, 267, 391 • Tel: 020 8994 8483

Whittard of Chelsea, Kingston
Neighborhood: Kingston, West London
Unit G9, The Bentall Centre, Kingston, Surrey, KT1 1TR

• Mon.-Wed. and Fri. 9:30am-6pm, Thurs. 9:30am-9pm, Sat. 9am-6pm, Sun. 11am-5pm • Nearest station: Kingston Railway Station • Buses: 111, 216, 281, 465 • Tel: 020 8546 9147

Whittard of Chelsea, Richmond
Neighborhood: Richmond, West London
12, Hill Street, Richmond, Surrey, TW9 1TN

• Mon.-Sat. 9am-6pm, Sun. noon-6pm • Nearest tube: Richmond • Buses: 65, 391, 419, 490, H22, H37, R68, R70 • Tel:020 8332 2669

Originally, the phrase Maids of Honour *referred to young women who were companions for a princess or other royalty at such palaces as Hampton Court (photo below). Today, the phrase is linked to a venerable tea room in Richmond, where the recipe for its famous tartlet is a well kept secret.*

"The bakery has been part of Richmond life for almost three
centuries, although the present shop is a mere 120 years old.
The tartlets after which it is named are said to have been
christened by King Henry VIII when he discovered Anne
Boleyn and her 'Maids of Honour' eating them from a silver
platter at Richmond Palace."

The Original Maids of Honour

Neighborhood: Richmond
288 Kew Road, Kew, Surrey, TW9 3DU

After walking around Kew Gardens, you will need a cup of tea to revive you,
so leave the gardens by the main gates and walk to your left along Kew Road
and cross at the pedestrian walkway. You'll be face-to-face with the well
known cottage-style tea room. The cake counter displays the famous 'maids of
honour,' a sort of old English curd cheesecake. The tea room takes you back in
time, with its chintz, rose-printed curtains, wooden furniture, and fireplace. A
wooden dresser in one corner and blue decorative plates on the wall complete
the effect.

The bakery has been part of Richmond life for almost three centuries – almost
as long as England's tea drinking history – although the present shop is a mere
120 years old (opened in 1887). The tartlets after which it is named are said to
have been christened by King Henry VIII when he discovered Anne Boleyn and
her Maids of Honour eating them from a silver platter at Richmond Palace.

The choices for tea here are Darjeeling, Assam, Earl Grey, and English Breakfast, brewed with bags. The tea is served piping hot, and there is a generous
amount in each pot. The savory quiches are very good, and the feather-light
scones are very fresh. These are served with small jars of Tiptree strawberry
jam and a scoop of clotted cream in a glass dish. All cakes are made on the
premises, including chocolate éclairs, choux buns stuffed with whipped cream,
brownies, fruit tarts, chocolate roulade, and cream horns.

• Restaurant open Mon. 9:30am-1pm, Tues.-Sat. 9:30am-6pm. Tea served
Tues.-Sat. 2:30-6pm • Nearest tube: Kew Gardens • Buses: 65, 391 • Tel: 020
8940 2752 • Reservations not accepted • Major credit cards • Tea by the pot,
Afternoon Tea • £

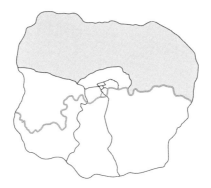

Northern Heaths and Hills

Camden, Hampstead,
Muswell Hill, Harrow-on-the-Hill

To the north of London's West End,
Camden leads the way to more rural areas
of Hampstead and Highgate. Here, heaths
and parkland surround smaller
communities that have retained their
village character. Shopping streets
offer a good mix of high class merchants,
including tea dealers, and walks in the
wide open spaces work up an appetite for
afternoon tea.

Kenwood House
Neighborhood: North London
Hampstead Lane, London, NW3 7JR

Kenwood House is an outstanding neoclas-
sical Georgian house set on the edge of
Hampstead Heath with an exquisite, quintes-
sentially English parkland spread out below.
With a gently sloping grassland and a lake,
a wonderful mixture of trees, and many
perfect views, it attracts hundreds of people
every weekend. Visits to the house are free,
and you are welcome to explore the many
meandering pathways and view sculptures by
Barbara Hepworth and Henry Moore.

When you become hungry or need a refreshing cup of tea, walk along the back terrace of the house to the Service Wing where the Brew House offers superb food and beverages. As you enter the Brew House from the courtyard of the Service Wing, you will see old-fashioned finger-point signs directing you to Cakes and Pastries, Tea and Coffee, Hot Food, Soup, Ice Cream, or Cashier. Collect what you fancy to eat and drink, pay, and then find a seat inside the lovely Brew House itself, where you can enjoy the painted panels on the wall and the twinkling glass lanterns. If you prefer, you may take your tray out into the terraced garden where large wooden tables spread around two sides of the Brew House. Huge white umbrellas will shade you from the sun.

All the cakes (there are chocolate fudge cake, prune and armagnac cake, and pecan, walnut and almond tarts), the scones, and the biscuits are made with stone ground organic flour. The meats are free range, and the eggs are organic. The teas (Assam, Darjeeling, Ceylon, Lapsang Souchong, Earl Grey, green and herbals) are loose leaf, supplied by William Martyn of Muswell Hill, and the menu is quite appetizing.

There is usually plenty of room, but this is a very popular spot at tea time, so you may need to scout around for a table. If you are visiting the house simply to enjoy the collection of paintings by Rembrandt, Vermeer, Turner, Reynolds, Gainsborough, Van Dyck, and Lely, or you planned a walk on Hampstead Heath, don't miss the Brew House. It is classy, attractive, and interesting, and the food is both healthy and delicious.

• Self-service restaurant open daily in summer 9am-6pm; off-season hours usually 9am-4pm • Nearest tubes: Highgate and then walk, or Golders Green or Archway and then Bus 210 • Bus: 210 • Tel: 020 8341 5384 • Reservations not possible • Major credit cards • Afternoon Tea à la carte • £

Yumchaa, Camden Market

Neighborhood: North London
East Yard, Camden Lock Market, Camden High Street, London, NW1

Yumchaa is run by a group of energetic and dynamic young people who encourage people to bring tea into their lives to create a sense of well-being and healthy living. The name of the shop has a double meaning. In Chinese, *yum chaa* means 'to make or to have tea.' The Yumchaa website puts an additional twist on the word: "At Yumchaa, we have one core desire: to make tea (Chaa) that tastes Yum."

The personalities behind the enterprise, Trinh Hoang, and her partner, Sean, work hard as a team, grab any opportunity to spread the word about tea, and involve people in an exciting way. They have a 'go for it!' spirit, always saying yes to a new approach. In their shop and market

The heaths of England are open areas covered with low shrubs or grasses, including heather, heath, and gorse. A wide range of birds are attracted to these habitats.

The Yumchaa branch at Camden is at the heart of a busy market that attracts thousands of people every weekend and throbs with life. There's no better antidote to the hustle and bustle than some of Yumchaa's tea. Yumchaa has additional locations in market stalls at St. James's Market and on Portobello Road.

stalls, they display teas so that customers can see, smell, and assess the leaf and other ingredients. Conversations with customers have an energy that is irresistible. People seem not to be able to walk past without stopping to ask questions and eventually to buy some tea to take home.

The Yumchaa teas are unusual flavored blends of black, green, rooibos, and white teas. Each goes by a clever and intriguing name – Sweet Secret, Notting Hill, Chelsea Chai, Mango Sunrise, Adventure, Ooh-la-la, Caramel Sweetheart, Enchanted Forest, Ginseng Guardian, and many more. The Yumchaa branch at Camden is at the heart of a busy market that attracts thousands of people every weekend and throbs with life. There's no better antidote to the hustle and bustle – either to enjoy on the spot or take home – than some of Yumchaa's tea. Yumchaa has additional locations in market stalls at St. James's Market, Leadenhall Market, and on Portobello Road.

• Fri.-Sun. 9:30am-6pm • Nearest tube: Camden, Mornington Crescent • Buses: 24, 253, 88, 27, 134, 168 • Tel: 07782 162896 • Tea shop serving and selling flavored loose leaf teas and infusions • www.yumchaa.co.uk • Check with banker's card, cash • £

Shopping Sites for Tea Lovers

Infuse Tea Ltd.
Neighborhood: Harrow-on-the-Hill
19 Roxeth Hill, Harrow-on-the-Hill HA2 OJY

Infuse Tea Ltd. offers courses in Japanese on tea and sells a fine line of tea gift products.

• www.infuse-tea.co.uk • Tel: 020 8426 8064 • Contact via e-mail: asteward@infuse-tea.co.uk

Martyns
Neighborhood: North London
135 Muswell Hill Broadway, London, N10 3RS

This lovely, old-fashioned grocery shop was opened in 1897 by the grandfather of current owner William Martyn. An emphasis on helpful

Martyns is a lovely, old-fashioned grocery shop opened in 1897 by the grandfather of current owner William Martyn.

101

family service and courtesy has continued through the decades. The façade of the shop is everything that storefronts used to be – lovely lettering and a generous window filled with appetizing goods. It gives a good solid feeling that invites you to walk inside.

There's no disappointment. The shelves are stacked high with top quality cakes, biscuits, jams, dried fruits, nuts, spices, and sweets. The teas, which are packed in simple, classy cartons, include English Breakfast, Earl Grey, Assam, Lapsang Souchong, Ceylon, Darjeeling, green, and herbals.

Due to recent requests from customers, William is in the process of adding new ones to the list. All Martyn's products are available by mail order. At Christmas, you can order a hamper that is packed full of selections from throughout the shop.

• Mon.-Wed. and Fri. 9:30am-5:30pm, Thurs. 9:30am-1pm, Sat. 9am-5:30pm • Nearest tubes: Turnpike Lane then Bus 144, Archway, Highgate then Bus 134 or 43 • Buses 134, 43, 144 • Tel: 020 8883 5642 • Grocery selling loose and bagged teas • www.wmartyn.co.uk • Major credit cards

Whittard of Chelsea, Hampstead
Neighborhood: Hampstead, North London
41 Hampstead High Street, London, NW3 1QE

A few steps from Hampstead tube station and surrounded by smart delis, clothing stores, and wine shops, you will find a bijou branch of Whittards offering a carefully arranged selection of gifts, seasonal specials, and loose leaf and bagged teas. There's not much room to move inside the store, but staff members manage to squeeze an amazing number of products onto the shelves.

• Mon-Sat. 9:30am-6pm, Sun. 11am-5pm • Nearest tube: Hampstead • Tel: 020 7433 8569

A Royal, Crooked Day Trip

The Crooked House of Windsor Cafe-Tea Room (photo opposite)
52 High Street, Windsor, Berkshire SR4 1LR

Windsor Castle is an easy day trip out of London and a short drive from Heathrow Airport. After seeing its recently refurbished state rooms, famous doll house, and King George's Chapel, you can take a stroll through the nearby shops and stop for a cup of tea in a famous architectural curiosity. The Crooked House is a unique venue that serves traditional British food at a reasonable price. It boasts an extensive range of loose teas. The menu includes a lavish Victorian style afternoon tea and a scrumptious selection of cakes.
• Open everyday from 9:30am-6pm • Tel: 017 5385 7534 • www.crooked-house.com • £

The Orangery

To Tea Or Not To Tea

A refresher course on the various ways, brews, and times to enjoy tea and accompaniments in true British fashion.

Afternoon Tea

Described on some menus as a *set tea* or *full tea*, afternoon tea is an elegant, light meal accompanied by a choice of freshly-brewed teas served by the pot. A pot of tea is included in the price of the set tea, and no extra charge is made for additional pots served during the meal. Often, a pot of hot water is provided to dilute strong tea. Formally presented all-at-once on a tiered server, or à la carte, courses consist of several kinds of crustless finger sandwiches or other savories, followed by scones, and then sweet treats such as petits fours, cake, cookies, and éclairs. Traditionally served between three and five o'clock, some venues offer afternoon tea from lunch on. Hotels often offer a glass of champagne, especially when tea time spills over into the cocktail hour. (In this guidebook, the phrase afternoon tea is capitalized only when it is a menu item for a specific tea room.)

Black Tea

Black tea is fully-oxidized. Freshly-plucked green leaves are withered and then twisted or rolled to release and oxidize natural enzymes. Finally, the leaves are dried to become the familiar black leaf noted for its rich, full-bodied brew. Most British teas are blended to accept the addition of milk (not cream).

Blended Teas

Teas from a variety of estates are often combined to ensure a quality product under changing agricultural conditions. Flowers, fruit, herbs, spices, and scented or flavored oils may be added. Earl Grey is an example of a blended tea.

Chai

Masala chai (*chai* rhymes with *tie*) is a drink made with ground black tea infused with milk, sugar, and a variety of spices such as cardamom, cinnamon, cloves, ginger, and black pepper. In India, it is traditionally drunk from a disposable pottery cup.

Clotted Cream

This decadent accompaniment to scones and jam is made in Cornwall, Devon, Dorset, and Somerset. It is made by scalding cream in a double boiler and has an average butterfat content of 63 percent.

Compressed Tea

Green, black, and puerh teas are sometimes pressed into cakes and blocks of different shapes. These may be bowl-shaped, ball-shaped, flat and round, flat and triangular, flat and rectangular, or other combinations. For tea preparation, some of the cake is broken off and brewed in boiling water.

Cream Tea

In the past, this term could easily cause confusion to those not familiar with our habit of tucking into scones and clotted cream, and visitors from abroad would sometimes try to add the clotted cream to

their tea before being instructed otherwise by watchful waitresses. A Cream Tea usually consists of two scones served with jam and clotted cream and, as with an Afternoon Tea, the pot of tea is included in the price. It is very hard to pinpoint when this set tea became a tea-time standard, but it almost certainly originated in the western counties of Britain where clotted cream was regularly made from the rich milk that Cornish, Devon, Somerset, and Dorset cows produce. There are many different ways to eat a scone, but normally, the scone is cut in half horizontally, then each half is spread first with jam and then with clotted cream. Or one picks up the first half of the cut scone, adds a little jam and then a little clotted cream, and takes a bite. More jam and cream is then added for the next bite and so on until the entire scone has been devoured.

Crumpet
This traditional British tea fare is a small, round unsweetened bread cooked on a griddle, toasted and served with butter and jam.

Green Tea
Green tea is the brew's oldest form. The leaves are steamed, rolled, and dried, not oxidized. Chinese varieties tend to be more mellow than "grassy" Japanese teas.

High Tea
Frequently confused with afternoon tea, high tea originally was a working class meal that developed to feed hungry workers when they returned from long, tiring days in factories, mills, mines, and offices. When they arrived home around six in the

evening, the family would sit down around the kitchen or dining room table and replenish lost energy with meat pies, homemade breads, cheese, ham, cold meats, salad, toasted muffins and jam, cakes, and puddings. A large pot of strong black tea sat in the middle of the table to quench everyone's thirst. In its early days, it was known as *meat tea* or *great tea*.

Oolong Tea
This partially-oxidized tea comes from China and Taiwan. The flavors vary but are generally complex and gentle, sometimes fruity, and always fragrant.

Pudding
Anything synonymous with dessert in Britain is often called a pudding, even if it is not in the least bit like a pudding. Favorites are sticky toffee pudding, bread pudding, and plum pudding. Remember that Yorkshire pudding is served with roast beef and is not a dessert.

Puerh
Puerh teas are aged teas that are allowed to mature (sometimes for as along as 30 years) in order to develop an elemental, earthy flavor. The leaves are withered and then heaped in piles while still moist. The bacterium in the leaves causes a chemical reaction that gives the teas their distinctive aroma and taste. At the end of the process, the tea is dried and packed loose or pressed into cakes of different shapes and sizes. Puerh tea is said to be very good for you, especially if you have high cholesterol.

Rooibos
South African *Rooibos (ROY-boss)* or *Red Bush tea* is a caffeine-free herbal infusion, high in Vitamin C and antioxidant properties. It is thought to relieve insomnia, headaches, nausea, asthma, and allergies.

Tisane
Tisanes (tih-ZAHN) are brewed with herbs, flowers, fruit, roots, berries, bark, or the leaves of any plant other than *Camellia sinensis*. They do not contain caffeine. Peppermint, chamomile, and ginger are common herbal tisanes. Strawberries, apples, blueberries, and other dried fruits make delicious fruit infusions.

Water Temperature
Water temperature plays a very important role in the production of a good cup of tea. One easily remembered rule is: the lighter the tea, the cooler the water; the darker the tea, the hotter the water. The following water temperatures are recommended.

White tea and green teas - 165 - 185° F (73-85° C)
Oolong teas - 185-200° F (85-93° C)
Black and puerh teas - boiling

White Tea
White tea, which is prized (and often pricey) is made from young tea buds that are plucked before they open, then steamed and gently dried. The curled buds have a silvery-white color and brew a straw-colored liquor. Originally grown in the Fujian province of China, white teas are now also produced in Sri Lanka and Darjeeling. The liquor is pale like champagne and the flavor is soft, smooth, and slightly sweet.

Tea in the City: London
An index to sipping and shopping

Alphabetical list of tea rooms and lounges

Algerian Coffee Store (Soho) 76
Aspreys (Mayfair) 58

Ceylon One (Southeast London) 87

Drury Tea and Coffee Company (Covent Garden) 77

East Teas (Southeast London) 87
Emma Bridgewater locations
    Fulham 93
    Marylebone 67

Fortnum & Mason Food Hall (Piccadilly) 47

Harrods Food Hall (Knightsbridge) 23
Harvey Nichols Food Hall (Knightsbridge) 24
H. R. Higgins (Mayfair) 48

Infuse Tea Ltd. (Harrow-on-the-Hill) 101

Martyns (North London) 101
Minamoto Kitchoan (Piccadilly) 60

Selfridges Food Hall (West End) 68
Silver Vaults (Holborn) 77

Tea House (Covent Garden) 79
Thomas Goode (Mayfair) 61
Twinings (Strand) 79

Whittard of Chelsea T-Zone locations
    Carnaby Street (Chelsea) 69
    Covent Garden 80
Whittard of Chelsea locations
    Battersea 93
    Bayswater 31
    Buckingham Palace Road (Victoria) 38
    Chiswick 96
    Coventry Street (Piccadilly Circus) 81
    Ealing 96
    Hampstead 101
    Kensington High Street (Kensington) 31
    Kings Road (Chelsea) 31
    Kingston 96
    Knightsbridge 31
    Moorgate (The City) 82
    Oxford Street (West End) 69
    Putney 93
    Regent Street (Central London) 81
    Richmond 96
    Strand (Central London) 82
    Victoria Station (Victoria) 38
    Wimbledon 93

Yumchaa, Leadenhall Market (Soho) 82
Yumchaa, Portobello Road Market (Royal Boroughs) 31
Yumchaa, St. James's Market (Piccadilly) 62

On the Tea Trail in London
(sites connected to tea history)

Holidays in England and Wales

The following dates are legal holidays,
when most banks are closed.
New Year's Day (Jan. 1)
Good Friday
Easter Monday
May Bank Holiday (first Monday in May)
Spring Bank Holiday (last Monday in May)
Summer Bank Holiday (last Monday in August)
Christmas Day
Boxing Day (Dec. 26)

Additional photographs courtesy of The Bentley (pg 19), The Milestone Hotel (pg 25), Mandarin Oriental (pg 30), The Goring Hotel (pg 35), Sofitel St. James (pg 37), The Connaught Hotel (pg 44), Claridges (pg 46), H. R. Higgins (pg 48), Four Seasons Hotel (pg 50), Le Meridien Piccadilly (pg 52), Park Lane Hotel (pg 54), The Ritz (pg 55, back cover), Sotheby's (pg 56), Aspreys (pg 58), Hyatt Regency London (pg 66), The Montague on the Gardens (pg 72), Royal Opera House (pg 72), Savoy Hotel (pg 74), Waldorf Hilton Hotel (pg 75), Yauatcha (pg 78), Marriott County Hall (pg 86), and Aquasia (pg 90).

Also available from Benjamin Press:

Tea in the City: New York
Tea in the City: Paris
The Great Tea Rooms of Britain
The Great Tea Rooms of America
The New Tea Companion

www.benjaminpress.com

JANE PETTIGREW
Author

Jane Pettigrew gained immediate respect as an author and tea expert when her first book, *Jane Pettigrew's Tea-Time*, was published in England. The book was subsequently translated into French, German, Italian, and Finnish, and Jane followed it with nineteen other volumes on topics related to tea, food, and etiquette. Her definitive book on the history of tea in England, *A Social History of Tea*, was published by the National Trust of England. She also served as editor of the journal, *Tea International*, and has lectured about tea throughout Europe, Asia and the Americas.

A former tea room proprietor (Tea-Time in Clapham), Jane still revels in the pleasure of taking tea with old friends or convincing new acquaintances of the wonders of her favorite beverage.

BRUCE RICHARDSON
Series Producer and Photographer

Bruce Richardson spends much of his time educating Americans in the art of celebrating afternoon tea. As a writer, photographer, tea blender, and frequent guest speaker at tea events across the nation, he draws from his fourteen years of experience operating one of America's best-known tea rooms – the Elmwood Inn in Perryville, Kentucky. Bruce is the author of six books on tea, including *The Great Tea Rooms of Britain* and *The Great Tea Rooms of America*. He and Jane Pettigrew co-authored *The New Tea Companion* for the National Trust of England in 2005. He is a columnist for *Fresh Cup* magazine and a contributing writer to several tea-related

publications. Bruce and his wife, Shelley, are the owners of Elmwood Inn Fine Teas and Benjamin Press.

Benjamin Press
Managing Editor: Freear Williams
Senior Project Editor: Patsi Trollinger
Maps: Tom Sturgeon

Other books in this series:
Tea in the City: New York
Tea in the City: Paris